Death By Choice Versus Religious Dogma

HANI MONTAN

Copyright © 2012 Hani Montan

Author: Hani Montan
      Australia, NSW, Panania

Title: Death by Choice versus Religious Dogma
Edition: 1st ed.
Edited by CreateSpace

Printed by CreateSpace
7290 B. Investment Drive
Charleston, SC 29418
USA

Subjects:

> Euthanasia—religious aspects
> Assisted suicide—religious aspects
> Right to die—religious aspects
> Life and death, power over—religious aspects

National Library of Australia (CIP)-Dewey Number: 241.697
BISAC (category): non-fiction

Author's earlier books: *Thorny Opinion, Dads Gags*, and *Israel vs. America vs. the World*

ISBN (13): 978-1467983686 (pbk.)
ISBN (10): 1467973683

Library of Congress Control Number: 2011961793
CreateSpace, North Charleston, SC

Contents

Introduction

This book is written from an atheist point of view to counter the ultraconservative theologians and followers of pro-life and religious-right groups who try to stifle the debate on the legalization of euthanasia and assisted suicide. It is a call to action aimed at the silent majority that is often stepped on by the vocal religious minority that imposes a non-secular ideology on everyone else. It is about the removal of the religious barrier from the terminally ill who no longer can be helped by medical intervention and who are in unbearable pain.

It's about the privileges of people who choose either to continue living till their last breaths or to end their lives peacefully because they don't want to be burdens on their loved ones or constantly sedated by drugs. It is about alerting people about the danger of imposing religious dogmas on others, which can destroy the concept of secular democracy.

It is about the dynamics of the debate on euthanasia and assisted suicide being shifted by the religious industry from "power and influence" to "power and control." The religious industry is hell-bent on ordering everyone to live and die according to its oppressive ideologies and the dogmas peddled by religious demagogues. The debate is now in desperate need of an injection of realism and counteraction.

The book is not only about euthanasia and assisted suicide but about human rights and the freedom of individuals to choose how they want to die. It is about the privilege of committed religious people to choose to continue living till their last breaths by tolerating pain or palliative sedation. And it is about the privileges of others who choose to end their lives because of their unbearable pain or who don't want to live undignified, bedridden, a burden on their loved ones, or constantly sedated by drugs. It is equally about the privileges of terminally ill atheists who reject religious dogmas and don't see the merit of living in pain and being burdens on others but prefer peaceful and dignified ends to their lives.

Furthermore, euthanasia and assisted suicide are not only about the intolerance of pain or being a burden on loved ones or a fear of dying without dignity; they are also about the loss of autonomy, the loss of the ability to engage in activities that make life enjoyable, and the loss of the control of bodily functions.

Euthanasia and assisted suicide are issues that affect the whole of society and have a significant impact on family relationships. Chapter 1 provides a definition of euthanasia (including passive and active methods of ending life with the direct supervision of a doctor) and assisted suicide (a method performed by the patients themselves with advice from a doctor).

Medicine should never be influenced by religion to adopt as its primary objective the aggressive prolonging of life at all costs. Instead medicine should be guided by the concept of giving patients comfort and reducing suffering.

For doctors to discharge their responsibilities objectively, they must have clear, scientific definitions of death and brain death based on the loss of capacity for consciousness. These definitions should allow them to turn off a life-support system at the appropriate time. Furthermore, the Hippocratic Oath, which dates back to the fifth century BC and is attributed to Hippocrates, has evolved and been amended many times since. It is now due for an update to accommodate the questions of abortion, euthanasia, and assisted suicide. (See chapter 4.)

The book rejects the imposition of an outdated ideology and the religious dogma of "God gives life and God takes it away," especially in regard to the nonreligious and terminally ill who are near death and want nothing to do with religious slogans because their painful and temporary existences are unbearable. It is the expectation, in a secular society where religion and state are separate, that the imposition of religious ideals on everyone is not acceptable. Religious dogmas should not be allowed to control people's lives, as was the case during the Middle Ages, when religious leaders were the rulers and dictators of social and political life.

The people who adhere to the slogan "God gives life and God takes it away" and believe in the "sanctity of life" are entitled to their beliefs, and it is their choice and prerogative to die whichever way they want. A painful death might suit their spiritual commitment and their belief that earthly suffering is good for the redemption of the soul. Others who don't tolerate pain but prefer to prolong their lives by a few more days or months with palliative care and by taking heavy doses of tranquilizing drugs should also be entitled to their choices. It is also the prerogative of some others who believe in "divine healing" and "miracles" even though, as is often the case, their conditions don't get any better.

Dogmatic religious leaders' undemocratic stances are the main stumbling blocks preventing the legalization of euthanasia and assisted suicide. Common sense and the prevailing social attitudes should be used as guidance for legalizing the practice in all civilized countries and states (with strict guidelines), modeled on laws currently practiced in the Netherlands and Oregon, United States.

This book is an extension of thought expressed in my earlier book *Thorny Opinion* and reinforces and builds on arguments laid out in the books of Derek Humphry, Robert Orfali, Timothy Quill, Philip Nitschke, Ian Dowbiggin, Stanley Terman, Gerald Dworkin, and many others who have devoted their lives and energy to this good cause.

The book's objective is to motivate the silent majority into action to protect their threatened democratic and human rights. Hopefully readers will find it informative and analytical.

The Author

Hani Montan is an atheist and an Australian citizen. He is married and has two daughters and one granddaughter.

In 1966 he earned a master of science degree in civil and industrial engineering.

He has travelled extensively, including studying and working in Iraq, Russia, Australia, and Algeria. To keep abreast of social, managerial, and technical developments, he has studied many subjects including project management, public relations, environmental protection, social and political science, psychology, human relations, business administration, and philosophy.

Montan worked at Sydney Water as a project engineer and group leader and owned and managed a retail business.

The experience he has gained from working with people over many years and his long interest in politics and social studies have given him the motivation to write about many different subjects that might be useful to many readers. This book and his other books (*Thorny Opinion*, *Dads Gags*, and

Israel vs. America vs. the World) are available on Amazon.com in both paperback and e-book formats.

This book is an extension of the thoughts expressed in his earlier book *Thorny Opinion*, which dealt with social, political, religious, and environmental issues and euthanasia.

In his next book, he will deal with the subjects of narcissism and human relations.

His blogs on various subjects can be found on OpenForum.com.au by searching for Hani Montan.

Chapter 1

◆ ◆ ◆

Definitions And Discussion

◆ ◆ ◆

Euthanasia (Mercy Killing)

Euthanasia is the intentional termination of a person's life, usually but not always at that person's request, and usually in the context of major injury, terminal illness, and/or incurable suffering.

It is the practice of ending a life in a manner that relieves pain or suffering or ending a life considered less than worth living. The precise definition of euthanasia is "a deliberate intervention undertaken with the express intention of ending a life, to relieve intractable suffering." For example giving a patient a lethal injection or putting a plastic bag over his head to suffocate him would be considered euthanasia. Humane euthanasia must be painless, with minimum distress, achieving fast unconsciousness followed by a serene death. It must be reliable and irreversible. (For methods and pro-euthanasia organizations, see chapter 8.)

Euthanasia is categorized in different ways, which include voluntary, non-voluntary, and involuntary as well as active or passive. In many countries active euthanasia is usually considered criminal homicide, but voluntary euthanasia is legal in some progressive and truly secular countries.

Presently mercy killing is the most active area of research in contemporary bioethics and is vehemently opposed by ultraconservative theologians, especially the Vatican.

In his book *A Merciful End: The Euthanasia Movement in Modern America*, Professor Ian Dowbiggin states that euthanasia is one of the most controversial bioethical issues in many Western societies. The question of what physicians are allowed to do in caring for people at the ends of their lives is a recurrent theme on the moral agenda of public and political debate. Dowbiggin shows that, at least since the late nineteenth century, active euthanasia or mercy killing has been advocated as an acceptable policy. He outlines the motives and methods used since then. In the early twentieth century, euthanasia emerged as a public health topic and was presented as a human rights issue as well as a social benefit practice. Freedom of choice is considered part of the evolutionary process of the right to die. The current debate about the legalization of euthanasia and assisted suicide is an extension of this history and the history of organized religions. Dowbiggin argues in favor of individual autonomy and the cost savings associated with social engineering.

The patient autonomy and individuals' rights movements demand the right to die and death with dignity. To discredit the pro-euthanasia movement, opponents intentionally try to confuse the issue by attempting to equate voluntary with involuntary euthanasia, which are not equal. Involuntary euthanasia, as practiced in Nazi Germany to exterminate people, has nothing to do with the current debate. At the same time, proponents of euthanasia don't see the difference between passive and active euthanasia but in completely different contexts. Passive is when a doctor disconnects a life-support system from a patient to let her die when she has no choice; active euthanasia is when the patient has the choice and total control.

The debate is about modern medical advances and the use of life-prolonging technologies that can keep patients bedridden or in comas for months and years. Medical interventions and some diseases can leave some patients suffering unbearable pain. Some medications can ease the pain and suffering but occasionally they don't. Then the patient ends up in palliative sedation, which is another form of undeclared euthanasia.

Dowbiggin demonstrates that the commitment to relieve human suffering has a long history and that the issue of legalizing euthanasia tends to reduce its complexities. It is hard to argue against death with dignity, but disagreement still persists as to whether passive and active euthanasia are the same. Euthanasia is a medical, philosophical, ideological, and cultural subject. The ideology has a Darwinian origin relating to natural selection and evolution, which contradicts creationists' assumption of the existence of God and his ownership of human life.

Passive Euthanasia

Passive euthanasia is legal in many countries but without clear definition. The laws authorizing medical practitioners to withhold medical treatment or to switch off life-support systems that are keeping patients alive often lead to misinterpretation and uneven application. The switching off of life-support systems or non-treatment is often accompanied by giving patients narcotics for sedation to enhance peaceful death.

The absence of a uniform legal framework for the concept of terminating life or disconnecting life-support machines makes it difficult for doctors to discharge their responsibilities to their patients and the community objectively, which leaves the patients and the health system at a great disadvantage.

In addition to the need for a uniform legal framework, for doctors to discharge their responsibilities objectively, a clear scientific definition of death and brain death is required. Brain death should be defined as the loss of capacity for consciousness, which can trigger the termination-of-life procedure of turning off a life-support system and introducing sedation and dehydration at the appropriate times. This definition is to protect doctors legally and to safeguard against next of kin or legal guardian objections to terminate life on religious grounds, especially when some religious sects (without scientific basis) believe death is when the soul leaves the body and insist on keeping patients alive till the last breath.

Religious leaders hypocritically turn a blind eye to the practice of passive euthanasia, which is common in most Western hospitals, including in some religious private hospitals. Morally it is considered equal to euthanasia or physician-assisted suicide, which the religious hierarchy is vehemently against, especially the Catholic Church. Some theologians and their followers, especially in the pro-life and the right-to-life movements, don't see the practice of disconnecting life support from a patient as euthanasia even when it's done to patients who have no choice, for example when they are comatose or in a vegetative state. Instead they see evil in people who are terminally ill and in unbearable pain requesting a merciful and peaceful death.

The phrase *mercy killing*, with an emphasis on *killing* instead of *mercy*, is used to discredit the concept of euthanasia and assisted suicide. The termination of the life of a patient who has no prospect of survival and is in constant pain or has an awful quality of life and wants to die with dignity, humanely, and peacefully with medical and professional assistance should be classified as an act of mercy. Doctors should be freed from negative stigma and unreasonable legal shackles and be able to use their logic, scientific knowledge, and professionalism in respecting a patient's needs and choices. In the absence of a uniform legal framework for the concept of terminating life or disconnecting life-support machines, it is difficult for doctors to choose the best courses of action for their patients.

Current medical practice is designed for doctors to employ all extraordinary means to prolong the lives of the terminally ill, and when they fail they discard the patients to palliative care. The system of medical care is becoming inefficient and acting against the best interests of the patients, their devoted families, and the community at large. Furthermore, palliative care is very expensive and is not affordable by all, which in many instances creates a situation that gives the rich good deaths and the poor bad deaths.

Patients who decide not to live in a vegetative state or in constant pain, even if they might survive longer with palliative care, should be given the freedom of choice. The legal framework must aim at the removal of the stigma of "killing" by doctors, who are meant to serve humanity and not be subservient to the religious industry. Doctors should be free from religious and political interference. Their objective should be to advise the patients who are at the end of life and their families to allow them to make informed decisions. Ultimately, doctors should respect their patients' and the legal guardians' wishes.

It is common, in the majority of cases, that the doctor's advice and the mere consent of the next of kin or the legal guardian are all that is required to disconnect the life-support system to affect the death of a comatose patient or a patient with a minimal chance of survival. In most cases the course of action is determined by the doctor's opinion. Unfortunately, however, in some cases patients with no chance of survival are kept alive in comas for days, weeks, months, and even years. The gradual increase in the practice of passive euthanasia, however, is now proportional to the increase of health costs, the scarcity of hospital beds, and the change in social attitude.

To overcome all anomalies and to clarify doctors' responsibilities and patients' rights, it becomes necessary to clarify the laws of passive euthanasia to allow doctors, in consultation with the next of kin or the legal guardian, to determine objectively the course of action that is in the best interests of the patient, the family, and the health system.

To achieve a positive outcome, it is necessary to abide by the patient's wishes enshrined in a document prepared earlier, when he or she was in good health and a normal state of mind. To simplify the implementation of passive euthanasia, citizens should be educated and encouraged to write their instructions in legally recognized documents to ensure their wishes are met if they become incapacitated and unconscious. (For more information on advance care plans and health care directives, see chapter 3.)

The Vatican Versus Passive Euthanasia

Observing the debate within the Catholic Church, one can easily conclude there is a huge gap between the ultraconservative theologians and the more practical ones. The conflicting views are adding to the confusion in the interpretations of the meanings of euthanasia and assisted suicide. This can be seen in Pope John Paul II's directives in 2004, when he spoke at the International Congress sponsored by the World Federation of Catholic Medical Associations and the Pontifical Academy of Life. His address, entitled "Life-Sustaining Treatments and Vegetative State," clearly stated removing the feeding tube of a disabled patient is immoral and amounts to "euthanasia by omission." He also rejected language used to describe disabled persons as "vegetables," calling such terms "degrading."

He spoke of the right of a sick person, whether awaiting recovery or natural end of life, to receive basic health care, i.e. "nutrition, hydration, cleanliness, and warmth, etc." He stressed that water and food, even when given by artificial means, are always considered *natural means* rather than *medical acts*. Since withdrawal of water and food can cause death by starvation and dehydration, it cannot be ethically justified.

The Pope rejected considerations about the "quality of life" often dictated by "psychological, social, and economic pressures." He acknowledged pressures placed on families to withdraw hydration and nutrition. He called for support of those families. He gave examples of programs and facilities that help patients and families and encourage medical staff and family teaming.

The Pope's remarks will take some time to be resolved, because many Catholic hospitals are continuing to follow the Ethical and Religious Directive for Catholic Health Care Services. These guidelines state that feeding tubes for patients in chronically vegetative states are "medical treatment" that can be continued or stopped based on the benefits and burdens for patient and family. The Ethical and Religious Directive requires that the patient's desire for no prolonged medical treatments must be communicated in advance. In New York state, that would mean specifying in a person's health care proxy what treatments he or she would forego and informing his or her health care agent, identified in the person's health care proxy document, of the patient's preferences when he or she can no longer make personal medical decisions.

The Pope specified nutrition, hydration, cleanliness, and warmth as **"ordinary care."** In America and in many other Western countries, it has become increasingly common to consider nutrition and hydration to be **"extraordinary care"** for some patients, usually those in extremely weakened physical conditions. Using the term *quality of life*, the medical profession bases the care decision on a judgment some would dare not make about another human being. In some countries provision of food and hydration is specifically defined as medical treatment. In some cases they even mandate doctors to withdraw hydration to patients whose potential quality of life is judged to render such treatment futile. In many countries' health directives, it is illegal for doctors to refuse to dehydrate patients to death if the patients or their legal guardians request it.

As can be seen, the Pope has created a division among Catholic ethicists, between the teaching of the Church and modern bioethics. Father John Paris, bioethics professor at Boston College, bluntly stated his defiance. He said, "I think the best thing to do is ignore it, and it will go away." He added, "It is not an authoritative teaching statement."

On the other hand, on July 13, 2011, in light of the Pope's directive, the lower house of the Italian legislature voted 278-205 to pass a bill that would definitively exclude the possibility of starving and dehydrating vulnerable patients to death. The Advance Directives Bill opens with a specific prohibition of euthanasia or assisted suicide and requires that patients not be denied food and hydration. No wonder Italy is going backward.

The national debate in Italy over advance directives and passive euthanasia follows the dehydration death of a young, brain-damaged woman, Eluana Englaro, in 2009. Despite the law against euthanasia, Eluana's father, Beppino Englaro, fought for ten years through the courts to have his daughter euthanized by dehydration. (For more discussion of religious dogmas, see chapter 5, and for more detail on Eluana's case, see chapter 7.)

Active Euthanasia (Voluntary)

Voluntary euthanasia could be achieved by self-delivery under supervision of a doctor with the doctor's prescribed medicine or the doctor can take an active role and administer a direct injection. Supervision and direct participation of a doctor make it more advantageous than assisted suicide, in which a doctor is not always present. In assisted suicide, if the patient requests that a doctor be present, the law prohibits the doctor from participating directly.

Active euthanasia is when a doctor, at the voluntary, expressed wish of a patient, causes the death of the patient by lethal injection or by any other intentional method to terminate life. The patient's request must be voluntary, explicit, and carefully considered, and it must have been made repeatedly. Moreover, the patient's pain and suffering must be unbearable and without any prospect of improvement or survival. It is a merciful and intentional termination of life and an active acceleration of a good death. It is the best way to pass away peacefully and serenely for terminally ill patients who are in persistent pain and nearing the ends of their lives.

Under current laws in the majority of semi-secular Western countries, this is considered a homicide. On the other hand, a few progressive, secular countries like the Netherlands, Luxembourg, and Belgium have legalized and administered active euthanasia under strict guidelines. In these countries the implementation of euthanasia laws has proven to be successful in achieving humane outcomes for terminally ill patients and in giving peace of mind to their families. (For laws and safeguards in countries where euthanasia and assisted suicide are legal, see chapter 6.)

Unfortunately, in countries that pretend to be secular, where religion and state are meant to be separate, the issue of freedom of choice and laws relating to euthanasia and assisted suicide are dictated by the religious industry and obeyed by gutless and opportunistic politicians. These countries are directly or indirectly influenced by a minority of unelected but vocal religious leaders and the pro-life and religious-right groups who are trampling on the human rights and freedom of choice of the majority. This is despite the fact that over seventy percent of their population and sixty percent of doctors are in favor of legalizing assisted suicide.

The irony is that in many countries, pain relief administered by a doctor that may shorten or end a patient's life is considered normal medical practice. It is called *palliative sedation* and usually entails heavy doses of morphine for controlling constant pain. Hypocritically, palliative sedation is a common practice in many hospitals and hospices owned and operated by religious establishments, especially the Catholic Church. The practice is considered a form of passive euthanasia while the religious industry considers it as part of terminal care and not euthanasia. Who are they kidding?

Physician–Assisted Suicide

This differs from euthanasia in its application of the termination of life, which is achieved by the patient and not the doctor. The doctor knowingly and intentionally provides a person with the knowledge or means (or both) required for committing suicide, including counseling about lethal doses of drugs, prescribing such lethal doses, or supplying the drugs.

A doctor can prescribe a lethal dose of specific medicine such as morphine or barbitals for the purpose of causing death. He can also set up the lethal dose through a machine that can be activated by the patient when the doctor is not present. The machine is designed to enable the patient to trigger a switch for delivering the lethal injection. Alternatively, the patient can take the lethal dose orally, as a capsule or a liquid, such as secobarbital or pentobarbital. (For laws and safeguards, see chapter 6, and for methods, see chapter 8.)

The practice of assisted suicide is legal in Oregon, Washington, Montana, Luxembourg, Belgium, and the Netherlands, but unfortunately not in other so-called free countries where the majority of people favor its legalization. The majority of people in Western countries consider themselves individualists rather than conformists. It is a paradox: the promotion of individualism is the key to these countries' futures, yet they are controlled by outdated conservatism and reactionary religious-right ideologies. This is when freedom of choice and human rights principles should be adopted as a prerequisite for individuality to triumph over conformity.

Freedom of choice and human rights should not be crushed by the use of emotive and manipulative words like *killing* as a substitute for *mercy* when describing the humane act of assisted suicide. The moral crusaders, the religious-right groups, and the pro-life movement don't understand that the majority of people are now more scientifically educated, especially in the concepts of evolution, astronomy, and genetics, which don't accord with their creationist ideology of a religious God based on metaphysics and speculation. The majority of educated people believe in themselves rather than in a dictator in the sky. These enlightened people support the argument "If there is a right to life, there must be a right to death."

There is huge ethical inconsistency in imposing the views of a vocal, fanatical minority over the moderate, silent majority. The ethical inconsistency is highlighted by the denial of the elementary human right to have access to information about one's life and its termination. The principles of right to death and right to have access to information should be the minimum for an individual living in the twenty-first century, especially in the educated, civilized world. It is the responsibility of any society to give its desperately ill patients serene, legal, and painless deaths if they wish, instead of driving them and their loved ones into despair and an illegal course of action or, in many cases, committing a painful and agonizing suicide.

A simple question should be asked: what rights do conservatives, conformists, and ideologues have to deny suffering people the freedom to choose to end their lives painlessly if they wish? These proud individuals not only want to end their own suffering but also the suffering of their immediate families and their loved ones who share their agony.

These were the same guiding principles that led to transforming assisted suicide from a crime into medical treatment in the Netherlands, Belgium, Luxembourg, Oregon, Washington, and Montana. In the Netherlands, Belgium, and Luxembourg, both euthanasia and assisted suicide are legal.

In Switzerland, although euthanasia and assisted suicide are illegal, assisted suicide is punished only if it is performed for a selfish motive. Assisted suicide there can be performed without the involvement of a physician. The irony is that, on the other hand, under Swiss law euthanasia is still considered a "murder upon request by the victim." Although the debate in Switzerland is still raging, a positive outcome in resolving the conflict and legalizing euthanasia may not be in the distant future. (For more on Switzerland's euthanasia laws, see chapter 6.)

Legalization of assisted suicide in these progressive countries and states puts to shame all other semi-secular, non-secular Western countries, where ultraconservative theologians dictate to the politicians. Opportunistic and gutless politicians who are scared of losing the backing of an influential minority of vocal religious leaders should be exposed and booted out of the government. Progressive countries and states also put to shame the religious leaders who want to lead their countries back into the Middle Ages, when ignorance was dominant and when they had power and control over all aspects of social and political life.

The advocacy of the logical principle "If there is right to life, there must be right to death" must triumph over the unsustainable dogma "God gives life and Gods takes it away." (For more on religious dogmas, see chapter 5.)

Suicide

Suicide is the process of purposely ending one's own life. Religious and nonreligious people view suicide differently and in accordance with the influence of religion on their culture. In many countries' cultures, the religious establishments (Christian, Jewish, Islamic) tend to view the killing of oneself as ungodly and negative, and sometimes as crime. One myth about suicide is that it is the result of mental illness. Some people, under certain circumstances, see suicide as honorable, in cases such as protesting against political persecution (for example hunger strikes that end up in death); as part of battle or resistance (for example the Japanese suicide pilots during World War II, the Vietcong heroism during the Vietnam war, and the Islamic suicide bombers); or as a way of preserving the honor of individuals or their families. However, in the majority of cases, people commit suicide because they are tired of living or are suffering from depression or incurable and painful ailments that are beyond current medical science.

By not accepting the right of patients who are living in psychological or physical agony to choose assisted suicide for peaceful and serene death, religious leaders indirectly accept or turn a blind eye to suicide, no matter how ungodly, cruel, and painful it could be. This is a dilemma that hypocritical politicians and religious fanatics appear to be happy to live with rather than contradicting their undemocratic, illogical, and inhumane dogmas. Despite their tragic cruelty, suicide and attempted suicide are not criminalized, leaving people with the power to pursue them.

The religious industry doesn't care about people who are tired of life or suffering from incurable and painful ailments who commit suicide by jumping off bridges, shooting themselves, slashing their wrists, hanging themselves, or taking strychnine or cyanide. Furthermore, the religious industry accepts that suffering patients are legally allowed to refuse medical treatment, which usually leads to a painful transition from the time of termination of the treatment to the end. For example, the week between disconnecting a dialysis machine from a patient who is refusing the treatment and

death is one the most painful transition periods if the procedure is not accompanied by narcotics or other sedatives.

These inhumane methods of ending life are extremely
fearful, distressful, and very painful. In many cases they are of
long duration without certain outcomes. In cases of suicide,
when a first attempt fails, another attempt is made and another, until the horrible death is achieved. This is what the
religious industry ignores when arguing against the peaceful
and serene termination of life of a desperate and terminally
ill patient who has a few months, weeks, or days left to live
in emotional and physical agony.

Nearly one million people worldwide commit suicide
each year, and there are from ten to twenty million suicide
attempts annually. In America about 30,000 people report-
edly kill themselves each year. Suicide is the eighth leading
cause of death in males and the sixteenth leading cause of
death in females. The higher frequency of completed suicides in males versus females is consistent across the life
span. Additionally there are the suicidal tendencies of self-
mutilation and other self-injurious behaviors including self-
burning, head-banging, and cutting parts of the body.

The least these suffering people deserve and have the
right to accurate information on how to end their lives painlessly. Unfortunately, these desperate people are deprived of
their democratic rights of access to information about safe
methods to end their lives. Instead they rely on less reliable
information found on the Internet or refer to a book like
HowDunit: The Book of Poisons by Serita Stevens and Anne
Bannon. The book names poisons and what areas they affect, such as the heart, breathing, or muscles. It tells the
reader about the reactions to poisons and how long they
take to take effect. It identifies poisons and groups them by

symptoms, forms, household, plants, poisonous animals, and so on. It also details history and where to find antidotes. Above all, it tells readers how to create their poisons.

There is more information in a book by Dr. Geo Stone entitled *Suicide and Attempted Suicide*. In it Stone details step-by-step many methods of suicide and their consequences. The book shows readers the many ways to die and the many ways to live. It deters the ones who need deterring and assists others who fail to get help from others, especially the ones with depression or mental illness who are excluded from any consideration of physician-assisted suicide. This is when untreated, long-term depression could be as painful as an advanced terminal illness.

The information in these books, however, is no substitute for a doctor's legal prescription of eighteen grams of Nembutal or information where to get it (places in China, Mexico, Peru, Oregon, and so on). Suffering people deserve serene death instead of brutal and uncertain attempted suicide.

Article 19 paragraph 2 of the International Covenant on Civil and Political Rights states that everyone shall have the right to freedom of expression; this right shall include freedom to seek, receive, and impart information and ideas of all kinds, regardless of frontiers, either orally, in writing, or in print, in the form of art or through any other media of his or her choice.

The freedom to seek and receive information is an essential element that should be included in the subjects of euthanasia, assisted suicide, and suicide. As it stands patients suffering unbearable pain and nearing the end of their lives who want to die peacefully and with dignity are deprived of reliable information on the best method of achieving their wishes. This is the least that can be done in countries where assisted suicide is not legal.

This is what the ultraconservative theologians and their fanatic followers are contravening—the International Covenant on Civil and Political Rights.

Human Rights And Human Dignity

The charter of the United Nations calls for recognition of the inherent dignity and the equal and inalienable rights of all members of the human family as the foundation of freedom, justice, and peace in the world. These rights are derived from the inherent dignity of the human person in accordance with the Universal Declaration of Human Rights. The ideal of free human beings enjoying civil and political freedom and freedom from fear and want can only be achieved if conditions are created whereby everyone may enjoy his or her civil and political rights as well as his or her economic, social, and cultural rights. It is the obligation of all states under the Charter of the United Nations to promote universal respect for and observance of human rights and freedoms.

Euthanasia and assisted suicide have been the subjects of much moral, religious, philosophical, legal, and human rights debate for too long. At the core of this debate is how to reconcile competing values: the desire of individuals to choose to die with dignity when suffering and the need to uphold the inherent right to life of every person. The position of international human rights law with respect to voluntary euthanasia is not explicit or clearly defined. Article 6(1) of the International Covenant on Civil and Political Rights (ICCPR) provides: "Every human being has the inherent right to life. This right shall be protected by law. No one shall be arbitrarily deprived of his life."

The impact of article 6(1) on voluntary euthanasia and assisted suicide raises a number of questions including the scope of the right to life, the interpretation of *arbitrary* deprivation of life, and the definition of life, in particular when life ends.

As can be seen, the world is being very dishonestly misled into thinking the subjects of euthanasia and assisted suicide are full of controversy and in need of endless debate. Those directly responsible for this unfortunate state of affairs are a small collection of vocal, theological, ultraconservative religious leaders who are hell-bent on keeping control over life and death no matter the cost. Their loud arguments are absorbed by politicians and medical associations—victims of the religious power and influence that has evolved into religious power and control.

Furthermore, many medical professionals are hiding their real favoring euthanasia and assisted suicide because of the religious industry's fear mongering and lies. Religious leaders often use blackmail tactics for silencing enlightened doctors and politicians by attaching unfavorable tags to them. Religious leaders have always exploited people's uneasiness regarding death and their fears of going to hell. Their invention of the nonexistent heaven and hell is one of biggest earners for their business, and they would hate to lose the underlying concept of reward and punishment.

The spread of apathetic feeling suits some politicians and medical associations, as they are infected with it and react to it without regard or moral obligation to any but themselves. The consequence of religious influence and control on the silent majority is that decisions regarding euthanasia and assisted suicide are left up to the medical profession and fearful politicians. This puts doctors in the unenviable position of having to deal with inadequate and non-uniform laws that leave suffering patients at a great disadvantage. It renders politicians powerless to make suitable laws for their nation.

Theologians' dogmatic belief in immortal souls is causing many suffering patients who don't have the power or the means to end their miserable lives to die in agony. Although it is incomprehensible to many, it is understandable that some people get comfort from a belief in a supernatural being. This, however, should not impinge on the rights of non-believers, agnostics, the less dogmatic, and other enlightened people.

Impinging on the rights of others was exemplified in an edict from Pope John II in January 2003. Archbishop Wilson sent the edict to members of the Irish parliament and directed it to all Catholics worldwide. The document instructed all to follow Catholic teachings and obey the Pope in their personal lives. It also instructed all Catholic politicians to take the dogma to the floor of the parliament. This offensive instruction made the Vatican the dictator of legislative agendas for the whole world to follow. The edict went beyond the impinging on the rights of others; it was a clear indication that the Church was not only interested in influence but after total control of the legislative agenda.

This sort of dangerous instruction is in total conflict with the concept of a multicultural, secular society. Members of parliament are meant to leave religious dogma at the door instead of applying it so critically. A secular society and its politicians should be guided by science and rational thinking instead of religion based on conjecture.

Instead of following the dogmatic and ultraconservative Pope, it is more appropriate to follow the guidance of Bertrand Russell, who wrote, "What we need is not the will to believe but the will to find out." It is also more appropriate to follow the guidance of Clarence Darrow, who said, "The realm of religion is where knowledge leaves off, and where faith begins, and it has never needed the arm of the state for support, and wherever it has received it, it has harmed both the public and the religion it would pretend to serve."

It is worth noting that the European Convention on Human Rights gives a person the right to die. However, according to Britain's highest court, the right to life does not include any right to self-determination over life and death, since the provisions of the convention were aimed at protecting and preserving life. On the other hand, English law already acknowledges that people have the right to die. The Suicide Act (1961) made it legal for people to take their own lives. Everyone has the right to die because human rights imply death is a private matter when it causes no harm to others. Therefore, the state and the religious-right groups have no right to interfere.

Every person has inherent dignity and value. Human rights help people recognize and respect this fundamental worth in the individual and in others. Human beings are independent biological entities. They have the right to make decisions for themselves provided they are not inhibited by subjective ideology and not impinging on others' rights. Therefore, they have the right to control their bodies and lives and should be able to determine at what time, in what way, and by whose hand they will die. Human beings should be as free as possible without unnecessary restraints on their human rights.

Imposing the subjective religious dogma of "people belong to God" constitutes a direct infringement on others who believe in themselves rather than in God. Secular people, agnostics, atheists, and even many religious people who believe in themselves take responsibility for themselves and their loved ones who deserve to be free from the burden of constant care and emotional suffering. These people take into account their obligations to society and balance their individual right to die against any bad consequences that it might have for the community in general.

Countries where euthanasia and assisted suicide are not legalized are in breach of human rights by forcing their terminally ill and desperate citizens to go through many barriers to achieve reasonable outcomes to their predicaments. Citizens who are terminally ill and in pain are forced to travel overseas to buy euthanasia drugs or to progressive countries where the practice is legal, seeking doctors who can assist them with euthanasia or assisted suicide. This adds further stress to their unbearable conditions. Furthermore, it is unfair to the terminally ill who don't have the means or cannot afford the burden and cost associated with such journeys. It is an anomaly: hypocritical religious leaders and gutless politicians are happy to live with at the expense of suffering people.

The question should be asked: what right has anyone, because of his or her own religious faith to which others don't subscribe, to demand that others must behave according to specific religious rules?

Ultraconservative theologians accept the legality of suicide and passive euthanasia, including palliative sedation in some of their own hospices. At the same time, they are willing to discriminate against those terminally ill patients who would like to be assisted to die peacefully but do not have the means to do so. To deny people their right of choice implies individuals don't know what is right for themselves. To be denied the right to make life-and-death decision is a blight on democracy and secularism. (For more on human rights and the right to die, see chapter 5.)

Finally, the following is a manifesto by Derek Humphry that was published on March 23, 2009, titled "Liberty and Death: A manifesto concerning an individual's right to choose to die."

In a spirit of compassion for all, this manifesto proclaims that every competent adult has the incontestable right to humankind's ultimate civil and personal liberty—the right to die in a manner and at a time of their own choosing.

Whereas modern medicine has brought great benefits to humanity, it cannot entirely solve the pain and distress of the dying process.

Each person deals with death in their individual way. Which way is determined by their health, their ethics, and personal living conditions.

The degree to which physical pain and psychological distress can be tolerated is different in all humans. Quality of life judgments are private and personal, thus only the sufferer can make relevant decisions.

Persuasion or provocation to the act of self-killing are deplorable and should be punished according to relevant laws. "Suicide" no longer being a crime, it is unacceptable to prosecute well-meaning people for "assisted suicide."

Medically hastened death by request should be made lawful as it is now in the Netherlands, Belgium, Luxembourg, Switzerland, and the American states of Oregon and Washington (each has different rules).

Choosing to hasten death by self-starvation and dehydration should be accompanied by palliative care. Electing to die by terminal sedation is also a choice provided it is freely made by the patient.

Advance Directives (Living Wills) and Durable Powers of Attorney for Health Care must be respectfully considered by medical professionals at all times.

Views on the dying process contrary to those expressed in this manifesto are respected, but must not trump the autonomy of the dying person's own decisions.

Freedom Of Choice And Quality Of Life

Everybody knows what they want and should have the freedom of choice to meet their own needs provided they don't encroach on others' freedom. Individuals act instinctively, influenced by the rules of nature. They respond to the world in accordance with their biology and their needs. They analyze the past and predict the future, which equips them to decide upon and undertake a course of action for their survival or demise.

Instincts have worked well since humans came to be—more so in the current comfortable and civilized environment that drives our human instincts using the evolved and well-developed thinking mind. The decision for one's demise could be construed as a mistake and in contradiction to the religious dogma of "God gives life and God takes it away." In this instance individuals should be answerable to God directly (if there is one) and, if they sin, be punished accordingly. These individuals should not be dictated to by ultra-conservative theologians pretending to act as gods who are hell-bent to control life and death. Religious leaders should not be allowed to dictate how to live and how to die or intimidate gutless politicians with religious dogmas when society and the system of government are meant to be secular and religion is meant for worshiping and the spirituality of people who need it and believe in it.

In a civilized country citizens are meant to be creative individuals rather than conformist zombies driven by a single ideology based on conjectures about God. Individualism is the key to the adoption of freedom of choice and human rights principles as a guarantee for a better future and a triumph over conformity.

It is a paradox that in Western countries, where individuality is the key to the future, zealot religious leaders are allowed to impose their outdated conservatism and reactionary dogmas.

The democratic rights of suffering patients and their families should not be trampled on. Human choices affect life; they form the present and future, relationships with others, and the way and quality of life. Although individuals have the right to commit suicide, they must also have the right to die painlessly, with pride and dignity. The alternative to the painless termination of one's life, when there is no medical help available, is for terminally ill people to commit suicide with unforseen consequences.

In 1989 a group of physicians concluded, in a report in the *New England Journal of Medicine*, that it would be morally acceptable for doctors to give patients suicide information and prescriptions for deadly drugs so they could kill themselves. Dr. Ronald Cranford, one of the authors of the report, publicly acknowledged this was "the same as killing the patient."

Euthanasia and assisted suicide, on the other hand, are not about private acts; they are about letting a doctor facilitate the death of a patient who chooses to die serenely and with dignity.

Civilized countries should not allow religious-right groups to inflict their worldviews on others. Given the right conditions, these fanatics, in the name of God, can take control and establish a fundamentalist dictatorship. This can be seen in the way they use God in almost every situation. The only thing that can stop them is the entrenchment of a genuinely secular system of government.

No nation in the world should allow the backward-looking ultraconservatives to govern.

Palliative Care

Palliative care is the practice of prolonging the dying process. It is not about cure; it is about symptom control. It can control pain in many cases but not the body debilitation, shortness of breath, nausea, and so on that drastically diminishes the quality of life. It is the stage that follows the failure of medical treatments and the transition into comfort care that eventually leads to the patient's death. Comfort care is when doctors shift their emphasis from aggressively treating the disease to treating the patient as a human being. This is the time when the traditional medical training of doctors is exposed as inadequate.

In his description of comfort care, Dr. Quill, in his book *Death and Dignity*, wrote:

> Comfort care involves distinct trade-offs and priorities compared to traditional medical care. In traditional medical care, increased suffering is reluctantly accepted as a side effect of treatment that is directed primarily at extending the patient's life. In comfort care, unintended shortening of a patient's life can be accepted as a potential side effect of treatment, provided the primary purpose of the treatment is to relieve suffering. The underlying religious and ethical principle is called the "double effect," which absolves physicians from responsibility for directly contributing to the patient's death, provided they intended purely to alleviate the patient's symptoms. It places considerable weight on the physician's unambiguous intent to relieve suffering and not to intentionally shorten life.

This arrangement has, to a certain extent, resulted in humanizing medical procedures and improved quality of life before death of some patients by treating them as humans instead of treating them aggressively for their underlying diseases. However, for many patients, death is the preferred option. Dying is part of life, and declining or withdrawing treatment is acceptable if it coincides with the wishes of the patient. The ethical issue of deliberately ending the life of a person who is terminally ill and in agony should be considered and his or her wishes respected. The practice of palliative and end-of-life care does not include euthanasia or assisted suicide even if it is requested by the patient. Interest in voluntary euthanasia is sparked by a need for assurance that pain and suffering are relieved and the individual's end-of-life decisions are respected.

Palliative care advocates pretend they can relieve pain by constantly giving patients heavy doses of painkillers and morphine injections. This doesn't remove the community's fear of ignoring individuals' rights to articulate their care preferences before crises, when they are no longer able to express their wishes.

Some patients nearing the ends of their lives may need and accept the compassion associated with palliative care (in hospitals, at home, or in hospice), which entails coordinated medical and nursing health services. Despite many of the patients' preferences to be cared for in their own homes by their own families, the majority end up cared for and dying in hospitals as huge burdens on the health system. Others are cared for by and become huge burdens to their families and loved ones, which adds to the patient's stress and feelings of guilt. All these situations come at a great cost to communities' and the country's economy.

Small numbers of patients are cared for and die in palliative care establishments (hospices), the majority of which are owned and operated by the religious industry for huge profit from patient contributions, insurance companies, and government subsidies. Cynics might say this profit is a good incentive for advocating palliative care. In some cases however, dying in the comfort of a hospice is better than dying in the intensive care unit of hospital where aggressive medical intervention is the norm.

Doctors often feel obliged, either ethically or legally, to treat a disease to the bitter end no matter how intensive or invasive the treatment or how hopeless its chances of success.

And patients don't consider themselves in a position to know their rights. They are not given the opportunity to consider their options until there are none left. After doctors fail to treat them, patients are often sent to palliative care establishments for comfort and pain relief. To prolong their lives by a few more days, weeks, or months, and without consideration of their wishes and the quality of the final stages of their lives, they are given strong doses of painkillers. Often these medications are insufficient to eliminate pain or restore the patient's desire for terminating his or her life serenely.

A major argument in favor of euthanasia and assisted suicide is when a patient is in great pain and has no desire to continue living. Despite the advances being made in the treatment of pain, palliative care still leaves the patient in a drugged and undignified state. In many instances families and friends of these patients are the driving force behind the desire for termination of life with **dignity** and they are the voice behind the legalization of euthanasia and assisted suicide.

Proponents of palliative care may say, "How do you measure **dignity**?" The simple answer is: give patients and their proxies the right to decide because they are the only ones in a position to judge, relative to their own perception, their feelings and circumstances. Alleviating pain temporarily doesn't solve the problem of emotional suffering and the depression that often accompanies physical conditions. In the majority of instances, bedridden and terminally ill patients need 24/7 care and feel undignified or as if they are huge burdens on their loved ones and the community. **Palliative care might suit some patients but not everyone.**

The following can be observed in some of the palliative care facilities that are managed and operated by the religious establishment, especially in areas where they have a monopoly:

- First, the religious industry doesn't take the moral high ground of charity and provide the care for free, which is a disadvantage to the poor majority.
- Second, often, gay people are not permitted there.
- Third, because of palliative care is very expensive and affordable only by some, it creates the problem of the rich getting the "good death" and the poor getting the "bad death." The poor are, as usual, thrown on the scrap heap, which contradicts the Christian slogan of "we are all born equal and die equal."
- Fourth, when the end of life nears, the common practice in hospices is slow death by palliative sedation, making the patient comatose with a continuous pumping of morphine. This practice often results in shortening life and the eventual death of the patient, which amounts to euthanasia by default. It is usually accompanied by withholding hydration and nutrition to prevent edema (the building up of fluid) of the lungs.

Yet, hypocritically, the religious industry consistently campaigns against euthanasia and assisted suicide and against the use of Nembutal, which is currently considered the best medicine for fast and serene death. (For more information on Nembutal, see chapter 8.)

In his book *Death with Dignity: The Case for Legalizing Physician-Assisted Dying and Euthanasia*, Robert Orfali, using the latest data from Oregon and the Netherlands to highlight the shortcomings of end-of-life management in America, compares the life of a patient in palliative care to terminal torture. He makes a compelling case for legalized assisted suicide. Furthermore, he adds extra dimension to the arguments against slippery slopes and the sanctity of life and questions the integrity of medicine with its high-tech interventions and palliative sedation. His data shows there is fifty-fifty chance patients will receive end-of-life palliative sedation in hospices, which, as stated earlier, amounts to euthanasia by default.

He also points out that in hospital intensive care units, many times people die while being treated aggressively and painfully to try to prevent their death. He makes the case that this aggressive treatment, in terminal cases, is more like torture. He advocates assisted suicide as a complementary method to palliative care as it is practiced in Oregon, which he considers to be the best system in America. Since legalizing assisted suicide, the state of Oregon has taken great strides to improve its end-of-life system.

Based on the experience of Oregon, Orfali strongly advocates the use of Nembutal as end-of-life medicine in palliative care-establishments. He wrote:

The Nembutal is your guaranteed delivery method for relieving unbearable pain. It protects you from the whim of hospices that do not provide palliative sedation. It protects you from being tortured in an ICU. You have peace of mind. You carry your delivery-from-pain mechanism with you at all times (*see below). You are not at the whim of a capricious and unpredictable system. Even with hospices, there's no way to tell in advance whether they will use palliative sedation even if you need it. The National Hospice and Palliative Care Organization's (NHPCO) numbers indicate that there's a huge disparity among hospices in the use of palliative sedation. With usage numbers ranging between 1% to 52%, obtaining palliative sedation in a hospice becomes pure luck of the draw. You'll need the Nembutal option to protect yourself from the vagaries of the system. Hopefully, you'll never have to use it.

*Orfali means that in Oregon you obtain a prescription and buy the Nembutal earlier than you need it, and use it if the hospice doesn't provide palliative sedation or when you decide it is time to say goodbye. (For more on Nembutal, see chapter 8.)

In his informative book, which contains useful statistics and analyses, Orfali examines unnecessary patient suffering caused by slow death and chronic disease. He believes some of the suffering can be easily managed if the system allows people to be informed about their end-of-life choices and how to become normal consumers of death. As it stands the system is unpredictable and lacks uniform application.

Another useful book, *Death and Dignity: Making Choices and Taking Charge* by University of Rochester professor of medicine and psychiatry Dr. Timothy E. Quill, is worthy of attention. Quill defines certain circumstances under which a rational patient should have the right to choose death and to enlist the aid of a physician to ensure "death with dignity." His empathetic exploration is a great help to readers in making informed decisions in tragic situations. (More information on Quill's book is in chapter 3.)

Chapter 2

* * *

An Atheist's Declaration

* * *

As can be inferred from the tone of my introduction and chapter 1, I am against religious dogmas controlling the political and social agendas in our civilized society, which is meant to have a secular system of government. Before proceeding with the rest of the book, for the purpose of transparency, I wish to make the following declaration and explain my atheism. This could be useful in assisting you to accept or reject my philosophy and my advocacy for the legislation of euthanasia and assisted suicide, which is vehemently opposed by the ultraconservative theologians.

My advocacy for legalizing euthanasia and assisted suicide, however, has nothing to do with my being an atheist; it has to do with my objection to a vocal minority of religious-right groups who want to impose their beliefs and will on everyone else and trampling upon my human rights and freedom of choice. As an atheist the stand I have taken should in no way impinge on the rights of the believers who find comfort in belonging to God and follow their own chosen paths. People have the right to believe in the sanctity of life and that God has created them and has sovereignty over them. I respect their beliefs, their human rights, and their freedom of choice and expect the same in return.

I object to the religious-right groups' undemocratic stand as the main stumbling block preventing the legalization of euthanasia and assisted suicide. These minority groups want everyone to live and die in accordance with their oppressive ideologies, which I think are in desperate need of exposure and counteraction by the silent majority.

My Mottos

First: I want to live when I am in good health and with a good quality of life. I *don't* want to live suffering constant pain or under palliative care or at all costs. This is the time when my sanctity of life ends and my freedom of choice begins.

Second: I am not made up in the image of God because I don't know what it is. I recognize my own image because it is real. The image of God that I read or hear about was invented by man and then turned it into a big business for a huge profit and the building of religious empires, complete with a huge institution, infrastructure and clergy power designed for indoctrination. God's image was meant to unite people when they were divided, but unfortunately it divided them more. Above all, there is no scientific proof of his or her existence.

Third: By virtue of believing in myths as absolute facts, the mind is usually blocked from analyzing and accepting logic. Religion therefore doesn't lend itself to reasoning and open-mindedness. It is in conflict with mankind's enquiring mind, which is constantly searching for answers and will not be satisfied with today's conclusion but strives for a better one tomorrow. Humans are motivated by curiosity to discover and to apply their discoveries to improve their lives and their chances of survival.

Fourth: Human behavior is driven by two main natural forces; the desire to avoid pain and the desire to gain pleasure.

Religious Fairy Tales

Through mind control of the naïve, the religious establishment has made a huge profit from their inventions of heaven and hell, the Virgin Mary, miracles, Noah's ark, the afterlife, the resurrection of Jesus, the second coming of Jesus, and so on.

Miracles and the Virgin Mary stories are unashamedly called *divine interventions*, which are only for good causes and never for bad ones. For example, if you die suddenly or if your children get sick or your mother gets breast cancer, the will of God is ignored. These are not miracles because in the eyes of an irrational, blind believer, God accepts only credit and never blame.

The invention of miracles can be illustrated by the way they create saints. Mary MacKillop was one of the last saints created because two patients prayed to her and "miraculously" got cured of their cancer. The next saint will be Pope John Paul II because another two patients are in the process of ensuring he will become one. Being an atheist I have no option but to be cynical. Their tricks can fool only the less informed and the blinkered believers.

(For more on Mary MacKillop and Pope John II, see chapter 6 of my earlier book, *Israel vs. America vs. the World*.)

About miracles generally, it is worth repeating what Scottish philosopher David Hume (1711-1776) wrote:

> A miracle is a disturbance or interruption in the expected and established course of things. This could involve anything from the sun rising in the west to an animal suddenly bursting into the recitation of verse. Very well, then, 'free will' also involves decision. If you seem to witness such a thing, there are two possibilities. The first is that the laws of nature have been suspended (in your favor). The second is that you are under a misapprehension, or suffering from a delusion. Thus the likelihood of the second must be weighed against the likelihood of the first. If you only hear a report of the miracle from a second or third party, the odds must be adjusted accordingly before you can decide to credit a witness who claims to have seen something that you did not see. And if you are separated from the 'sighting' by many generations, and have no independent corroboration, the odds must be adjusted still more drastically. Again we might call upon the trusty Ockham, who warned us not to multiply unnecessary contingencies.

Generally Hume defined a miracle as "a violation of the laws of nature." This definition entails that a miracle is beyond the productive power of nature.

It is worth noting the work of William of Ockham (1288-1348), an English scholastic and philosopher believed to have been born in Ockham, a small village in Surrey. He is considered one of the major figures of medieval thought and was at the center of the major intellectual and political controversies of the fourteenth century. He is commonly known for Occam's razor, the methodological principle that bears his name, which is: "When two explanations are offered, one must discard the one that explains the least, or explains nothing at all, or raises more questions than it answers." William of Ockham also produced significant works on logic, physics, and theology. It is believed he studied theology at the University of Oxford from 1309 to 1321.

It is also worth noting Hume's description in the *Natural History of Religion* (long after the invention of the one God):

> Monotheism is dogmatic and intolerant; worse, it gives rise to theological systems which spread absurdity and intolerance, but which use reason to corrupt philosophical thought. But since religion is not universal in the way that our non-rational beliefs in causation or physical objects are, perhaps it can eventually be dislodged from human thinking altogether.

Natural History of Religion has cemented Hume's reputation as a religious skeptic and an atheist.

The irony of religion is that it employs a good percentage of above-average, educated people who are engaged in the least productive sector of the national economy. It could be said it is even worse—it does more harm than good by fragmenting the nation while it is subsidized by the taxpayers.

Fairy Tales

One of the most successful fairy tales religions invented to convince the blind believers, was the linking of human spirituality to religion and God. They were able to link religious spirituality to Western civilization, which was based on mythologies that originated in the Middle East over 4,000 years ago. The path to spirituality should not be narrowed to mythologies but include a deeper understanding of individuals' personalities. Religionists promoted the idea that religion is the only source of spirituality and transcendence, when in fact these are psychological states of human intuition and perception and existed long before the invention of God and the emergence of the first religion. Intuition and perception are personality characteristics that relate to heredity and the environment and have nothing to do with religion. Heredity and the environment are natural, while religion is only an imposed ideology that can have limited influence on people's social environments. With the decline of religion, its influence on people is diminishing in tandem.

The worst fairy tale, on the other hand, is the story of Adam and the way he ate the apple and was fashioned out of clay by God. The funny part of the fairy tale is how, through no fault of his own, Adam was created with built-in sins and punished for them. For a start God gave him sexual desire, yet he was forbidden to lust for woman. The irony of this is his "free will," which God gave him (maybe as a bonus), could not prevent his sexual desire. (For the cynical: preventing an erection can only be achieved by medicine, castration, or, ultimately, divine intervention.)

On the other hand, this would have contradicted the other mythology of "go forth and multiply." I found it impossible to believe this religious mumbo jumbo and decided to avoid it at all cost along with many other fairy tales, especially the ones that assumed God spoke many languages, such as Aramaic, Hebrew, Greek, Farsi, Arabic, Latin, and so on. What a pity God couldn't speak English! Many of these languages were spoken in dialects by God's archangel Gabriel to the prophets and other selected people, like the Virgin Mary.

Here it is worth mentioning that God and Gabriel were able to speak but didn't know how to write; the many scriptures were written by an army of God's supporters many centuries later. However, exception should be made for the believers in the fairy tale that God engraved the Ten Commandments on two stones for Moses to take home to his people.

It is easy to imagine the mess, conflicts, and conquests caused by the many interpretations of what was said and transmitted between many generations before it was written down. Furthermore, and since then, it has been translated to many modern languages, which caused more conflicts resulting in accusations of heresy and sectarian violence.

It is easy to see that accepting religious ideologies and mythologies blindly, without questioning, means shutting down the brain from the natural and critical thinking processes. Accordingly, doubting or rejecting the idea of God is an essential step toward rational thinking and the expansion of mental horizons. It leads to understanding nature and the universe in reality rather than through a spiritual and mythical prism. The phrases "God's will" and "everything is in God's hands," for example, don't enter the atheist's mind because they mean "stop thinking, don't doubt, and don't ask."

One religious indoctrination tool is reinforcing the idea of God has created everything. This is when the existence of a religious God is not proven and cannot be proven by metaphysical and supernatural argument. There is no evidence of his or her existence. If God created everything, then it should be asked, who created God? It must be them—the clever ones, the religious empire builders. Their creation story claims Jesus is the son of God. Without this claim Jesus would have been a useless entity without any commercial value.

Then there is the story of the Virgin Mary, which can only be considered another fairy tale. A virgin birth is a myth manufactured by man. St. Luke, speaking of the parents of Jesus, mentions only Joseph and Mary. St. Matthew and St. James mention the brothers and sisters of Jesus. On reading conflicting mythologies, it becomes obvious Mary's virginity is a farfetched assumption suiting the blind believer who accepts the theologians' selective interpretation of the Bible as undisputed truth.

Modern people are forward looking, which is the opposite of religious backward looking, especially when religion is based on myths and is subject to many interpretations. When social progress and sophistication can be measured by people's attitudes toward science and technology, women's participation in social and economic life, and the secular system of government, secular wisdom is adopted as a guide for the nation. On the other hand, backwardness is measured by the dominance of religion in citizens' daily lives; the absence of women in social and economic life; belief in the afterlife, miracles, and mysticism; and the wide spread of superstitions.

Indoctrination

Despite having been brought up in an environment dominated by the Christian Orthodox Church, I came to the conclusion that religion is not for me. I gave it up at the age of fourteen and became involved in politics at the age of fifteen. I doubted the religious stories of Adam and Eve, Moses parting the sea and Jesus curing the blind, walking on water, raising the dead, and so on. If Jesus (as a god) could solve all these things miraculously, then why couldn't he solve simple problems, like stopping suffering, diseases and natural catastrophes from killing so many people, especially innocent children? If he is so passionate and so powerful, how come he made humans, which he supposedly created suffer so much? What is the purpose of creating such a world in the first place? Why he as a god had to suffer at the hand of the Jews?

Ironically I am still waiting for a reasonable answer instead of nonsensical BS based on religious absolutism. Theologians' most common answer is, "Never doubt the Bible. If you do, you are not Christian and you'll end up in hell for eternal punishment." Doubting the Bible is heresy, and they are not kidding.

Despite their threats, however, I chose hell and lived happily ever after, distinguishing the good from the evil without their BS. To be more cynical, I have to add that since all religions state if you are not one of theirs, you will go to hell. Accordingly, an assumption could be made that *everybody* will go to hell.

With my further development, it became obvious to me that religious leaders are patriarchal and often do the opposite of what they preach. They relegate women to secondary roles despite the fact that women have achieved a great deal in political, social, emotional, and economic equality with men outside the religious circle. Women's modern journey commenced in the eighteenth century, during the Age of Enlightenment, while the world was still waiting for religious leaders to become enlightened. Don't hold your breath, especially when these leaders are still following St. Paul's direction of "wives obey their husbands" and when the Vatican's recent revisions put the ordination of women on par with child abuse. This revision is coming from a church where the sexual abuse of children by its clergy is common.

As for the religious leaders' hypocrisy, this chapter is insufficient to describe it. Similar to euthanasia and assisted suicide, they advocate natural death as an ethical course, yet they accept unnatural and aggressive life-prolonging medical procedures, especially for themselves, by not allowing their God to take them away naturally at the appropriate time.

Another hypocrisy is telling people to give generously to help the poor while they give away little of their own. Instead of giving the donations to the poor, they use them to enrich themselves and enlarge their empires. Furthermore, they have the temerity to ask the poor for contributions so God will forgive their sins.

Religious leaders keep reinventing themselves to keep the continuity and viability of their businesses going. People who are totally committed to religion through guilt are convinced they need to confess their sins daily and constantly repent. In the process they donate money to the church so God can forgive their sins.

It is worth noting that earlier, during the Middle Ages, some very smart, ultraconservative theologians decided to make money from people's sins by selling indulgences (tickets to heaven) to people without requiring them to confess or repent. The money was used to build bigger churches and a more powerful empire.

Through religious traditions and ceremonies filled with song and dance, the religious industry has been able to create a euphoric atmosphere that makes people susceptible to entrapment and conditioning that makes them too generous toward religious causes. The commercialization of religion has been essential for its growth and survival. Many centuries ago religious leaders understood money was power and power meant control. Control still means everything, mentally, socially, and politically. The biggest control religious leaders have over the less-informed is their invention of heaven and hell—the concepts of reward and punishment aimed at a naïve section of the community, which is their power base.

To wake up from the religious nightmare, all one needs is a bit of doubt about and no fear of this invented hell because it doesn't exist—neither does heaven. Doubting is the first step toward mind liberation and individualism.

Religious leaders' lust for money can be summed up by how they collect donations from churchgoers: "Please place your donation in the envelope along with the name of the deceased person you want remembered." My father before me came to the conclusion that religion is about money, power, divisiveness, and control and should be fought. Without the divisiveness of religion, people should be able to develop their own ethics and principles and live by them. The differentiation between good and evil, as well as high moral values and a belief in social justice can be learned from many sources other than mythologies or hypocritical priests. Their hypocrisy is historically enshrined in the biblical insurance policy of "do what they say and don't do what they do." When priests cannot abide by religious teachings, it is a confirmation that religion is too idealistic to follow and is in conflict with human nature and natural instincts. Atheists and agnostics, being more open-minded, avoid religious subjectivity and its conflicts and are more suited to acquire and pass on to the next generation objective values without being dogmatic.

Religion traps people in the box of subjectivity at an early age. This makes it difficult for less-informed people to become free thinkers. Setting oneself free from something one didn't choose in the first place requires deep thinking. It is ultimately the individual's knowledge, self-analysis, and critical thinking that can get him or her out of the box and to freedom.

To achieve their objectives, religious leaders employ mass psychology and brainwashing techniques on their constituency. They indoctrinate children early, when they are most susceptible, especially through the taxpayer-subsidized religious schools, which enjoy tax-exempt status. This is how the leaders ensure the continuity of their enterprise. Their strategy of indoctrinating children can be highlighted by the remarks attributed to Ignatius Loyola the founder of the Jesuits, five hundred years ago, who said, "Give me the child for seven years and I will give you the man."

The indoctrination of children is a form of abuse. Secular society should never sacrifice its most valuable assets to the religious industry. It is ridiculous that some of the so-called civilized countries so heavily subsidize religious schools for such a negative outcome: the triumph of conformity over individuality, which retards children's creativity and produces the herd mentality, benefiting the religious industry at the expense of society. This can only happen because of religious activism and control over opportunistic politicians who fear losing votes as a result of religious backlash. Religious leaders, for their own survival, achieve their objectives by entangling religion with politics to allow them to use religion for lobbying purposes. In the process they render the secular system of government and democracy meaningless.

The religious industry spreads fear and insecurity—fear of God, fear of the unknown, fear of final judgment and going to hell. These are the tools they have used for many centuries in their endeavor to control human emotions and behaviors.

Through their subjective and manipulative interpretation of the scripture, they instill in people's minds that their brand of religion is the only truth, despite the ideological truth being relative. (The ideological truth can be one thing to one person and the opposite to others.) In the process they create sects, religious intolerance, and conflicts. The ultimate outcome, as we have witnessed, is sectarian fragmentation of the world. It is impossible to credit any one religion or any one god as true when there has been so many throughout human history. None has a greater claim to credibility or reliability than any other. Every claim has its fanatic supporters. They can't all be right.

One thing is certain, as history shows and as described by Friedrich Nietzsche: "Every church is a stone on the grave of a god-man. It does not want him to rise up again under any circumstances."

It is also possible that the Bible has nothing to do with the supernatural and miracles. That could be simply an error caused by writers and readers who could not see beyond the metaphor and didn't know that language has many meanings.

Mysteries and the Soul

Mysteries

My scientific background, which I have acquired through university education, experience, and interaction with enlightened people, has entrenched my atheism on intellectual grounds. The more I learned, the easier it became for me to observe how religious leaders indoctrinate people along traditional lines that disallow any doubt about God and scripture, which is in total conflict with the scientific approach based on doubt and not accepting the status quo. For example religiously committed people will never question the Trinity and are compelled to believe it blindly. They believe without asking the question "how can it be that God was the father, the son, and the Holy Spirit and after the son died, he went to heaven and sat on the right hand side of his father?" It is blasphemy and heresy to doubt or question this proposition, but for an atheist and any scientifically minded person, it simply doesn't make sense.

An attempt was made to explain it in Corinthians 15:24: "Christ is currently reigning at the right hand of God, and waiting for all his enemies to be placed under his feet. And after he has 'destroyed all dominion, authority and power,' he will hand over the kingdom to God the Father." John 1:14 says, "There is certainly no doubt that Jesus' existence is physical. He did not cease being man after he was resurrected, but instead, in the incarnation he 'became flesh and made his dwelling among us for eternity.'"

If you don't understand this mumbo jumbo, you are not alone. Understanding the Trinity is no small thing. It took the church almost 400 years (and several heresies) to come to an agreement on what is meant by God the father, son, and Holy Spirit. So this answer may take some rereading to understand fully—or it may never be understood. The Trinity is a mystery humans cannot understand; so is the claim of the existence of God. Similarly religion as a whole can only be understood (or pretend to) by people with blind commitment.

The promotion of mysteries is the foundation of the religious enterprise.

The Soul

In religion the soul is connected to the idea of the immortal essence that is left over at death and referred to as *ghost* or *spirit*. The idea dates back to the ancient Assyrian and Babylonian beliefs of the eighth century BC. It was used in the commemoration of life and the afterlife.

Many religious interpretations have followed since. Catholics define the soul as the innermost aspect of being human, or the principle of life that which is of greatest value in people, that by which they are most especially in God's image. *Soul* signifies the spiritual principle in man. All souls, living and dead, will be judged by Jesus Christ when he comes back to earth. The souls of those who die unrepentant of serious sins or in conscious rejection of God will, on judgment day, be put forever in a state called *hell*.

The Catholic Church teaches that the existence of each individual soul is dependent wholly upon God: "The doctrine of the faith affirms that the spiritual and immortal soul is created immediately by God."

Orthodox Christians believe that after death the soul is judged individually by God, and then sent to either paradise or hell. Further interpretation of *soul* by various Christian sects and other religions gets complicated; researching this can confirm to a sophisticated reader that it is all futile nonsense. This is especially so when some Bible scholars refer to St. Paul, who said that the body wars against the soul and that "I buffet my body to keep it under control." This is ignoring the fact that the mind controls the body and the only war is within the consciousness of the mind.

According to creationists, each individual soul is created directly by God, either at the moment of conception or at some later time. Among Christians there is uncertainty regarding whether human embryos have souls and at what point between conception and birth the fetus acquires a soul and consciousness. This uncertainty causes many Christian fanatics to impose control over women's bodies and declare war on abortion and its legalization.

Other Bible scholars have better described the soul as the *personality*. However, personality cannot be an immortal object because, as these scholars define it, the soul is the immaterial part of mental properties.

Personality is better defined as a byproduct of heredity and the environment—both social and natural. Personality components are intelligence, emotional intelligence, social intelligence and wisdom, which is a byproduct of knowledge and experience. Personality is a byproduct of something else. It is illogical for any of its parts to end up in heaven or hell.

Others consider *soul* a synonym for *mind*, where the psyche is more physical. Advances in neuroscience mainly serve to support the mind-brain identity hypothesis, showing the extent of the correlation between mental states and physical-brain states.

On the other hand, science places the soul in the realm of metaphysics, a type of philosophy or study that uses broad concepts to help define reality and our understanding of it. Metaphysical studies generally seek to explain inherent or universal elements of reality that are not easily discovered or experienced in our everyday lives. As such they are concerned with explaining the features of reality that exist beyond the physical world and our immediate senses. Metaphysics, therefore, uses logic based on the meaning of human terms rather than logic tied to human sensory perception of the objective world.

The laws of physics underlying everyday life are completely understood, and there's no way within those laws for the information stored in our brains to persist after we die. If a claim is made that some form of soul persists beyond death, the questions to be asked are: Of what particles is the soul made? What forces are holding it together, and how does it interact with ordinary matter?

Attempting to make the metaphysics of the soul into science doesn't work, since there is no scientific proof of its existence. It is an imaginary part of some people who believe in an afterlife and final judgment. For science the resurrection of Jesus and life after death have the disreputable connotations of an existence of past lives, reincarnation, and ghosts. They are fantasies with no controlled, experimentally verifiable information that satisfies the scientific standard. It is not possible to justify the claim that some form of consciousness persists after the body has died and decayed into its constituent atoms.

It is interesting to imagine that billions of individual souls are ending up aimlessly floating in the galactic space. Worse still, the traditional Christians believe in the resurrection of the body, which is when the word of consecration are uttered that the person becomes the body and blood of Christ. In some sense we will be there as continuing persons. In other with a new heaven and a new earth with all the good things that we've done will be incorporated into the new heaven and new earth. Can anybody solve this puzzle? Can any theologian explain such a mumbo jumbo? What happens when we die if we're buried or cremated or donated our bodies for scientific research? How can a person on eating a wafer and having a sip of red wine becomes the body and blood of Christ? Is this a placebo or religious opium? They believe it because the man who told them that was also the son of God. He supposedly said, "This is my body. This is my blood," and they prefer to listen to him and take his word without thinking.

Science versus Religion

It is appropriate here to repeat Christopher Hitchens's ironic remarks about religion and how it poisons everything: "Everything we know about philosophy, we first learnt because of religion. It deserves respect for being humanity's first attempt to make sense of everything, to discover knowledge. That was way back then. It's different—and dangerous—now." He added: "I think human civilization only begins when people separate religion from the state. Policing that frontier, making sure of it, is a huge thing, culturally and politically. You realize that any attempt to cross it is poisonous—in the sense of lethal."

Here it is worth adding what David Filkin wrote in his book *Stephen Hawking's Universe*:

> Following the crucifixion of Jesus, Christianity had rapidly eclipsed other belief systems throughout Europe. Its scriptures very clearly preached the creation of the world by God, with man and woman—in the form of Adam and Eve—on earth at the center of everything. And this was totally consistent with

the earth-centered universe described by Ptolemy. Increasingly, the Church became the exclusive patron of scholarship. Literacy was required for the study of the scriptures, and only the Church could afford to teach people to read. Eventually, all men of learning had to have the patronage of the Church if they wanted to study, and at the same time feed themselves and keep a roof over their head. This meant that scientists were also priests or monks, dedicated both to the study of science and the spreading of the Church's teaching. They unhesitatingly taught the story of God's creation of a Ptolemaic universe. Science and religion were as one.

Note that Ptolemy was an astronomer in the second century AD while the Bible was edited, sanitized, and canonized in the fourth century AD. With Ptolemy's model of the universe portrayed as a series of simple circular orbits with the earth at the center, he could only make the sun, the moon, and the planets circle the earth by adding complicated epicycles. However, his theory was challenged in the fifteenth century AD by a Polish priest named Nicholas Copernicus, who realized the sun was the center of everything instead of the earth. As we have seen, the advances of science and astronomy render the scripture (the foundation of religion) irrelevant. Since Copernicus, because of the intellectual threat posed to religion, conservative theologians turned against science. They understood that the laws of nature will ultimately render the supernatural fairy tales irrelevant.

The mythologies that religions are based on are no longer acceptable to knowledgeable and educated people. One of these mythologies is that the earth is 6,000 years old;

counting from the time it was created by God. This is embarrassing when compared with the scientific estimates of twelve billion years as the age of the cosmos and four and a half billion as the age of the sun and its orbiting planets, including the earth. (These estimates are subject to constant review.) It is more embarrassing when theologians reject all evidence of archeological and fossil finds, which in some instances date back millions of years, because they don't coincide with the Bible.

It is obvious that the founders of the religions were uneducated, had limited information, and had no idea about the natural order. Equally it is ignorant of us to follow them because there is not much to learn from what they thought. The knowledge they had is now out of date.

The mainstream holy books were written centuries after the death of their prophets, based on myths transmitted orally from one generation to the next as unsystematic stories. Therefore, the written texts can only be considered attempts at the writing of history. The speculation is then translated from Hebrew or Greek or Latin. Throughout the translations it can be seen that the so-called prophets were unable to predict the future. Furthermore, the texts are full of killing, bigotry, ethnic cleansing, and incitement to genocide, which are in total contradiction of "thou shalt not kill" and are systematically glossed over by modern theologians.

Apart from the above, it could be observed that the entrenchment of dogmatic beliefs often leads to superstition, which in turn leads to irrational thinking, which in turn leads to the inhibition of social and scientific progress. Furthermore, entrenchment of religious beliefs was and will always be the cause of fragmentation and continuous conflicts in the world, fueled by the historical contradictions contained in the Christian, Jewish, and Muslim so-called holy books and their many illusionary revelations, all of which subject to many interpretations. The fragmentation and divisiveness is aggravated by ultraconservative theologians who thrive on feeding their followers subjectivity and hatred to maintain their power and control. Historically religions were often the cause of conflict and destruction, and there will be no peace and harmony in the world until people decide enough is enough and abandon religions.

The danger of allowing religion to control politics is that it can gradually lead the country into social unrest. People should be vigilant and reject any politician who attempts to mix religion with politics. It is of paramount importance to prevent the political system from being exploited, influenced, or controlled by religious interests.

Historically, religion was often used as an anti-democratic tool to suppress freedom and human rights by placing God and ideology ahead of any other consideration. Religion and politics play pivotal roles in everybody's lives; therefore, it is everybody's responsibility to elect politicians with agendas of serving the silent mainstream majority rather than the vocal religious-right minority. To protect its democratic interests, the silent majority must shed its apathy and become more active and vocal in protesting manipulative, dishonest, and religiously dogmatic politicians. Above all, the silent majority must effectively use the ballot box to get rid of extremist politicians who represent vested interests and act as subservient to the religious establishment.

It is of paramount importance to remember that the social and political apathy of one generation can destroy the future and hope of the next generation. The silent majority, for its own survival, should become more active against and vigilant in regard to the influence and control wielded by religious-right politicians and fundamentalist, ultraconservative theologians.

The silent majority is equipped with knowledge and experience that allows it to sense the danger of fundamentalism and to arrive at logical conclusions that enable it to fight back against the forces of ignorance. Wisdom should always be the guide to humanity and the anchor to human survival rather than religious manipulation.

Here it is appropriate to repeat Professor Richard Dawkins's remarks: "I'm against religion that teaches people to be satisfied with non-explanations for things when in the twenty-first century we have extremely good explanations and we are getting better ones."

(For more on religion, see my earlier books, *Thorny Opinion* and *Israel vs. America vs. the World*.)

It is also appropriate to restate the American Atheists' mission statement:

> Your petitioners are Atheists, and they define their lifestyle as follows: An Atheist loves himself and his fellow man instead of a god. An Atheist accepts that heaven is something for which we should work now—here on earth—for all men together to enjoy. An Atheist accepts that he can get no help through prayer, but that he must find in himself the inner conviction and strength to meet life, to grapple with it, to subdue it, and to enjoy it. An Atheist accepts that only in the knowledge of himself and the knowledge of his fellow man can he find the understanding that will help to a life of fulfillment.

By logical deduction I came to the conclusion that self-belief will always trump the belief in any supernatural fairy tales that deal with subjective ideology, speculation, mysteries, and metaphors about God. Religion doesn't allow people to think or doubt; it is the absolute when the absolute doesn't exist except for existence itself or the universe, and when everything else is limited or relative. People cannot think through the religious absence of common sense, especially in its interpretation of wisdom as related to people seeking immortality through God. The lack of wisdom is for the ungodly, who face a miserable fate. Enlightened people define wisdom as knowledge, reasoning, experience, and conscious understanding of the world.

Religion is the opposite of science because science is founded on doubt and deals with realities, tested theories, verifiable information, and facts. In science, when different evidence and facts are presented, the conclusions are changed accordingly. A stark example of that is when Copernicus proved the earth went around the sun while the scripture said the opposite. The Vatican imprisoned Galileo for supporting Copernicus. The Church sensed that science would rock its foundation.

Another example is Magellan's circumnavigation of the earth and the earlier voyages of Vasco da Gama and Christopher Columbus, which finally established that the world was a sphere, which was the opposite of previously held beliefs. It is worth noting that later it was discovered that the earth is not a perfect sphere but is slightly pear-shaped.

In the near future, proof of the Big Bang theory based on the research to discover the subatomic particle will be forthcoming. On December 13, 2011, physicists at Cern said they had narrowed the search for the Higgs boson—the so-called elusive subatomic particle or the God particle (*see below) that is said to be the missing link in the standard model of physics and may confer mass. Scientists hunting the Higgs boson, believed to have played a vital role in the creation of the universe, have decided to turn up the power in their Large Hadron Collider (LHC) to try to prove its existence. According to the theory, the particle was the agent that made the stars, planets, and life possible by giving mass to most elementary particles, the building blocks of the universe.

For decades the standard model of particle physics has served physicists well as a means of understanding the fundamental laws of nature, but it does not tell the whole story. Only experimental data using the high energies reached by the Large Hadron Collider can push knowledge forward, challenging those who seek confirmation of established knowledge and those who dare to dream beyond the paradigm. Physicists are using the LHC to recreate the conditions just after the Big Bang by colliding the two beams head-on at very high energy. Teams of physicists from around the world then analyze the particles created in the collisions using special detectors in a number of experiments dedicated to the LHC.

It might be noted that the Higgs boson is theorized to be the force carrier of the Higgs field, which is thought to permeate the entire universe, endowing matter with mass. Only by using powerful particle accelerators like the LHC do scientists stand a chance of seeing these mysterious particles. In physics scientists describe the Higgs as having a huge mass of 125 giga-electron volts. If the Higgs does exist with this mass, then perhaps some more tricky universal mysteries can be resolved.

*Higgs boson is named after professor Peter Higgs, who came up with his theory about the boson particle during his work at the University of Edinburgh in 1964. The God particle is named after the title of Leon Lederman's science book on particle physics, *The God Particle: If the Universe Is the Answer, What Is the Question?* Lederman said he gave it the nickname because the particle is "so central to the state of physics today, so crucial to the understanding of the structure of matter, yet so elusive," but jokingly added that a second reason was because "the publisher wouldn't let us call it the Goddamn Particle, though that might be a more appropriate title, given its villainous nature and the expense it is causing." Lederman (born July 15, 1922) is an American experimental physicist and won the Nobel Prize in physics in 1988 for his work with neutrinos. In 1991 he became president of the American Association for the Advancement of Science.

Also forthcoming is proof by NASA scientists that liquid water was present on the surface of Mars in the recent geological past, raising the prospect that there might have been or still might be life in some form on Mars. If it is proven, then life on earth ceases to be the unique act of creation as being described in the Bible. Discovering any form of life on Mars or anywhere else in the universe will write God and religion out of the equation.

Further on the scientific horizon is the completion of the first draft of the entire human genetic code. If life as it is known is proven to be neither exceptional nor mysterious, the idea of God will be tarnished forever. Unlocking the secrets of life could mean stealing some of God's thunder.

All of the above thoughts and the Darwinian natural selection observations show there is no overriding purpose or design by God. Research is growing at an exponential rate and will leave religion behind. In the process it will prevent ultraconservative theologians from reinventing the concept of a God creator. In the past they were able to make people believe when only believers could make sense of their beliefs (or maybe pretend to), relying on inferences drawn from what was known of the material world.

However, one of the options left for them is to promote the concept of many gods or creators. The discovery of life beyond earth would mean sharing God and reconceptualizing the divine nature. Alternatively, God was a committee! The other option is to force religion on everyone. Indications of this are appearing through the emergence of the theocratic Tea Party in America, which is capable of taking the country to conditions that existed during Europe's Middle Ages.

Finally, I was recently impressed by a conversation between a very religious friend and his bright seventeen year old son who said, "Dad, the way science is progressing, in two hundred years all people of the world will become atheists."

Chapter 3

* * *

Advance Planning
for Death

* * *

In some instances patients with no chance of survival are kept alive in comas or in vegetative states for days, weeks, and even months, occupying emergency and hospital beds that could be used by other patients who may have reasonable chances of survival and recovery. Without a clear legal framework, the gradual increase in the practice of passive euthanasia is unevenly applied by hospitals and medical practitioners throughout the world. The practice is proportional to doctors' training, which is based on invasive medical treatment using modern technologies, the increase of health costs, the scarcity of emergency and hospital beds, an outdated Hippocratic Oath, and the change in community attitude.

As stated in chapter 1, modern and very expensive technologies, especially the application of invasive medical procedures and the use of an artificial breathing apparatus and feeding tubes, can keep a patient in a coma for years. In circumstances of this kind and in the absence of legal backing and proper guidelines, it is impractical for doctors to run an efficient health system or to make a choice in the best interest of the patient, his family, or the community. The problem with passive euthanasia is aggravated by the absence of a clear scientific definition of death and brain death based on the loss of capacity for consciousness and a clear definition of the appropriate time to withhold treatment or disconnect life-support systems, as well as the doctor's obligation to do so. However, in many hospitals in the civilized world, it is now common practice to authorize medical practitioners to withhold medical treatment or switch off life-support systems, allowing a comatose patient to die when there is minimal chance of survival.

There are laws or understandings that allow a patient to refuse treatment. Under such circumstances it is appropriate to explore the patient's feelings, possibly with the assistance of a qualified professional, and to address any issues that maybe resolvable. When the decision is influenced by temporary feelings of depression caused by unrelieved pain, the patient's treatment refusal could be unsustainable. It may be appropriate to negotiate with the patient an agreed plan of continuing treatment for the near future while acknowledging that sustained wishes for refusing treatment by a competent patient are ultimately paramount.

As it stands the practices of passive euthanasia and palliative sedation strip the patient's power to choose and give it to the doctor without proper supplementary medical and administrative scrutiny. This practice and the lack of monitoring of it compares badly to the proven legalized and methodical system of assisted suicide in Oregon and legalized euthanasia as it is practiced in the Netherlands.

Psychiatrist Dr. Stanley A. Terman, in his book *The Best Way to Say Goodbye: A Legal Peaceful Choice at the End of Life*, describes a method that gives suffering patients sufficient time to reconsider and have control over their decisions, with no residual effects if they change their minds about proceeding. This method maximizes the probability that others will honor the patients' advance health plans, especially if the patients are no longer able to communicate. Thus, Terman explains why everyone should create precise, unambiguous, strategic, written, and legally binding document.

Dr. Terman has clarified the many different aspects of the complex process of dying. It is about the family, medical, legal, financial, and religious choices one needs to make for the best hope of death as one would wish it. Based on his experience, he suggests everyone should complete three documents: a will, a financial power of attorney, and an advance health care directive (also called a *living will*), which includes the appointment of a surrogate with durable health care power of attorney. He also suggests the advance health care directive be entered into one's medical record by one's doctor.

Dr. Terman's comprehensive book is devoted to questions on the choice of dying. He offers many suggestions on how to make the dying process for patients peaceful. He presents a compelling case for a legal and peaceful alternative to physician-assisted suicide, which he calls "physician-aided, patient-hastened dying." He also provides a step-by-step guide for those who want to avoid lingering in the state of total dependency and indignity that can result from illness including Alzheimer's and other dementias.

It is interesting to know that there are laws in many Western countries and states that allow citizens to plan ahead for their preferences when they will not be able to decide for themselves in the event of major illness, an accident, or trauma. Some of these events may relate to a stroke, a brain injury, dementia that develops over time, and so on.

Before discussing any advance health care plan and directive, it is worthwhile to note the following descriptions of some diseases and events, such as accidents, strokes, or cardiac arrests that can leave patients with brain damage. Other events discussed are incurable dementia (such as Alzheimer's disease) that affects behavior, awareness, and consciousness; illnesses such as Lou Gehrig's disease (ALS); incurable cancer; and other illnesses such as reoccurring pulmonary embolism, malignant multiple sclerosis, and grade 4 glioblastoma).

These are only a small sample of the many events and debilitating diseases that, at their final advanced stages, may cause intolerable pain and suffering. It is usually at the advanced stages that a patient wishes for a peaceful and painless death. Some of these diseases may or may not apply to the subject of euthanasia or assisted suicide but are worth knowing.

Descriptions of Some Diseases

Gastric Cancer Stage Four

Gastric cancer is the second leading cause of cancer deaths around the world. Stage four stomach cancer means the cancer is advanced and has spread to other body organs through the lymphatic system. As with many other types of cancer, the outcome of stomach cancer depends on how advanced it is and when it is diagnosed. Because most stomach cancers are advanced when they are diagnosed, about fifteen percent of people diagnosed live for at least five years. About eleven percent live for at least ten years. Younger people tend to have longer survival compared to older people. In people over seventy with stage four stomach cancer, fewer than five percent live at least five years after they are diagnosed. Generally, doctors think a patient is lucky to live for two years after being diagnosed.

Its recurrent complications have debilitating effects on patients, especially after the initial radical gastrectomy, when surgical intervention is no longer feasible. In a rare manifestation of recurrent gastric cancer, patients show symptoms of upper-quadrant pain, nausea, and bilious vomiting. These disabling symptoms usually make oral food intake impossible and result in rapid deterioration of the general condition and impairment of the quality of life.

Chronic Arthritis

This refers to many medical conditions that affect the muscular-skeletal system, specifically the joints. It includes pain, stiffness, inflammation, and damage to joint cartilage, which cause joint weakness and deformities that affect the patient's daily functions. It is a major cause of disability and chronic pain and is not yet curable. In severe cases it has a major impact on a patient's quality of life.

People with more severe forms of arthritis can have serious problems with organs such as the kidneys, lungs, and heart. In a small number of people, some syndromes maybe associated with lymphoma, a cancer of the lymph glands. In others the conditions maybe associated with the body's immune system attacking the body's healthy tissues.

Stroke

Stroke happens when the supply of blood to the brain is suddenly disrupted due to either a blocked artery or a hemorrhage in the brain. Blood is carried to the brain by vessels called arteries; when one is blocked by a blood clot or plaque, or when the artery breaks or bursts; blood may stop moving through it.

When blood is stopped, the brain cannot get the oxygen it needs, brain cells in the affected area die, and the brain can become permanently damaged. Brain cells usually die within an hour from the beginning of the stroke but can survive, at times, up to a few hours after the stroke starts. Areas of the brain where the blood supply is reduced but not completely cut off can survive for some hours. The cells are in a state of shock and can either recover or die depending on what happens in the minutes and hours that follow. Without prompt medical treatment, the brain cells will die.

The brain controls all functions—moving, thinking, and speaking, and so on. When a stroke happens, the patient loses the ability to do things that are controlled by the brain. The way in which patient is affected depends on where in the brain the stroke occurs and the size of the stroke. For example someone who has a small stroke may experience only minor effects. Someone who has a larger stroke may be left paralyzed or in a coma. In some severe cases, the patient may die. Also in severe cases, life-support systems may be switched off when the patient has no chance of survival or will only survive in a vegetative state.

Multiple Sclerosis (MS)

This is a disease in which the nerves of the central nervous system (brain and spinal cord) degenerate. Inflammation causes the myelin—the semi-solid, fatlike sheath that surrounds the axon of the neuron—to disappear. Myelin provides a covering or insulation for nerves, which improves the conduction of impulses along them and is important for maintaining the health of the nerves. Consequently the electrical impulses that travel along the nerves decelerate and the nerves themselves are damaged. As more and more nerves are affected, a person experiences a progressive interference with virtually any sensory or motor (muscular) function in the body that is controlled by the nervous system, such as vision, speech, walking, writing, or memory.

The cause of multiple sclerosis is unknown, but it has become widely accepted that genetic, immunological, and environmental factors play a role. The selection of drug treatment or therapy is made after the patient with multiple sclerosis has been properly informed of the drugs' effectiveness.

There are different clinical manifestations of multiple sclerosis. During an attack a person experiences a sudden deterioration in normal physical abilities that may range from mild to severe. The attack sometimes referred to as an *exacerbation* of multiple sclerosis, typically lasts more than twenty-four hours and generally more than a few weeks, though rarely more than four weeks.

Sixty-five to eighty percent of individuals begin with relapsing-remitting (RR) MS, the most common type. In it patients experience a series of attacks followed by complete or partial disappearance of the symptoms (remission) until another attack occurs (relapse). It could be weeks to decades between relapses.

In primary-progressive (PP) MS, there is a continuous, gradual decline in a patient's physical abilities from the outset rather than relapses. Ten to twenty percent of individuals begin with PP-MS.

Those beginning with RR-MS can enter a phase where relapses are rare but more disability accumulates. They are said to have *secondary-progressive (SP)* MS. About fifty percent of RR-MS individuals will develop SP-MS within ten years. Over several decades most patients with RR-MS will experience a progression to SP-MS.

Progressive-relapsing (PR) MS is a type of multiple sclerosis characterized by a steady decline in abilities accompanied by sporadic attacks. There are cases of multiple sclerosis that are mild and can be recognized only retrospectively after many years, and there are rare cases of extremely rapid progression of multiple sclerosis symptoms (sometimes fatal) known as *malignant*.

Many of the symptoms, such as difficulty walking, muscle spasticity, weakness and fatigue, eye problems, emotional outbursts, pain, bladder dysfunction, constipation, sexual dysfunction, and tremors, are treatable with medicine or physical therapy. In severe cases of pain and tremors, however, drastic medical measures are often needed.

Lou Gehrig's disease (ALS)

Amyotrophic lateral sclerosis, or ALS, is a motor neuron disease of the nerve cells in the brain and spinal cord that control voluntary muscle movement. ALS is also known as Lou Gehrig's disease. In about ten percent of cases, ALS is caused by a genetic defect. In the remaining cases, the cause is unknown.

In ALS nerve cells (neurons) waste away or die and can no longer send messages to muscles. This eventually leads to muscle weakening, twitching, and an inability to move the arms, legs, and other areas of the body. The condition slowly gets worse. When the muscles in the chest area stop working, it becomes hard or impossible to breathe on one's own. There is no known cure for the disease.

The illness increases the need for food and calories. At the same time, problems with swallowing make it hard to eat enough. Sometimes breathing devices are used only at night; in some cases constant artificial mechanical ventilation may be necessary.

Over time, people with ALS lose the ability to function and to care for themselves. Death often occurs within three to five years of diagnosis. About twenty five percent of patients survive more than five years after diagnosis.

Glioblastoma Grade 4

Glioblastoma multiform is the most malignant form of brain tumor. Its symptoms include increasing mental dysfunction, seizures, persistent headaches, memory loss, muscle weakness, and evidence that there is pressure inside the skull including vomiting and protrusion of the blind spot at the back of the eye.

After initial treatment the tumor usually recurs within one to two years. Undergoing additional treatment after this phase has the potential of impacting quality of life and doesn't improve the survival rate. The average length of a patient's survival after undergoing surgery for recurrent grade four glioblastoma ranges from fourteen to thirty-six weeks.

Patients in this category cannot be cured. This is when family and doctors can decide to end the treatment as the patient is unlikely to live longer than six months, will be in agony, and will need constant care. If the palliative care option is chosen, the patient will need sedation that entails the continuous injection of a painkiller.

Pulmonary Embolism (Blood Clot in the Lung)

This is a sudden blockage in a lung artery usually caused by a blood clot that travels to the lung from a vein in the leg. It is often a complication of a condition called *deep-vein thrombosis*. Pulmonary embolism is a serious condition that can damage part of the lung because of a lack of blood flow to the tissues. This damage may lead to pulmonary hypertension (increased pressure in the pulmonary arteries) and cause low oxygen levels in the blood, which can cause damage to other organs in the body.

If a blood clot is large, or if there are many clots, or if they are left untreated, it can cause death. Most patients who succumb to pulmonary embolism do so within the first few hours of the event. Despite diagnostic advances, delays in pulmonary embolism diagnosis are common and represent an important issue. As a cause of sudden death, massive pulmonary embolism is second only to sudden cardiac arrest.

In patients who survive a pulmonary embolism, a recurrent embolism and death can be prevented by prompt diagnosis and therapy. Unfortunately the diagnosis is often missed because a patient with a pulmonary embolism presents with nonspecific signs and symptoms. If left untreated, approximately one-third of patients who survive an initial pulmonary embolism die from a subsequent embolic episode. When a pulmonary embolism is identified, it is characterized as acute or chronic.

Advanced Alzheimer's

Alzheimer's is an irreversible, progressive brain disease that slowly destroys memory and thinking skills and eventually even the ability to carry out the simplest tasks. It is the most common cause of dementia among older people. Dementia is the loss of cognitive functioning, thinking, remembering, and reasoning to such an extent that it interferes with a person's daily life and activities.

Alzheimer's disease is named after Dr. Alois Alzheimer. In 1906 Dr. Alzheimer noticed changes in the brain tissue of a woman who had died of an unusual mental illness. Her symptoms included memory loss, language problems, and unpredictable behavior. After she died, he examined her brain and found many abnormal clumps (now called *amyloidal plaques*) and tangled bundles of fibers (now called *neurofibrillary tangles*). Plaques and tangles in the brain are two of the main features of Alzheimer's disease. The third is the loss of connections between nerve cells (*neurons*) in the brain.

Tangles begin to develop deep in the brain, in an area called the *entorhinal cortex*, and plaques form in other areas. As more and more plaques and tangles form in particular brain areas, healthy neurons begin to work less efficiently. Then they lose their ability to function and communicate with each other, and eventually they die.

By the final stage of Alzheimer's, damage is widespread, brain tissue has shrunk significantly, and the plaques and the tangles have spread throughout the brain. People with severe or terminal Alzheimer's are usually unable to communicate and are completely dependent on others for their care. Near the end the person may be in bed most or all of the time as the body shuts down. In this stage the patient may become resistant to care and incontinent. Eating may become difficult, and the patient may have a reduced recognition of food.

Discussion

Most of the above situations and many others cause patients to lose control of their destinies. Worse is when the next of kin and doctors have no idea what a patient's attitude toward the quality of life she aspires to, the medical treatment she prefers, and the type of treatment she is offered.

Some patients may want all treatments possible, at all costs to them and the community. This perhaps is driven by hope or, in some instances, religious dogmatic belief in the "sanctity of life" or "life and death are in God's hands." Other patients may not believe in the existence a superpower in the sky controlling everything in the universe. These patients have more self-belief, value the quality of their lives dearly, and don't want to live in agony or be burdens to their loved ones. Instead they prefer to die serenely, with pride and dignity.

In any free and truly secular country, all patients, no matter what their beliefs are, must have total freedom of choice. To have their wishes fulfilled, everyone should make their preferences and choices clear to their next of kin and their doctors—long before a possible catastrophic event like permanent brain damage caused by a stroke or an accident. To ensure their rights and their near-death wishes are met, it is suggested that citizens consider the following before preparing their advance care plans and directives about their preferred treatments or death.

First: In an emergency your medical record is not available to the treating doctors. They have a professional obligation to take life-sustaining measures immediately. These could be overzealous and could leave you in a vegetative state, which you never wanted. The treatment, however, can change to coincide with your prior expressed wishes that you have included in your advance health directive before you became incompetent to make decisions for yourself. Second: Doctors are using extraordinary means to prolong the lives of the terminally ill and victims of major trauma like brain damage, which is not necessarily in the best interests of the patients or their devoted families, especially when the patients are in comas or vegetative states. Doctors are trained not to fail, no matter what and at all costs. (For the Hippocratic Oath, see chapter 4.) The only time they admit failure is when they refer a patient to palliative care, which means they have exhausted all possible treatments and what is left for the patient is to live the last days or months under the care of others.

Third: Generally the subject of an approaching death of an ill member of the family is considered extremely sensitive. Often, following a stroke or other major trauma, for sentimental reasons the next of kin and the rest of the family will decide to keep the terminally ill or comatose patient alive as long as possible. It might not be the patient's desire to survive in a vegetative state, but because he did not inform his loved ones of his wishes earlier, they will most likely act on hope rather than reality, even against doctors' advice. That advice may stipulate that the patient will be unable to self-feed or speak and will be permanently bedridden and require life support such as mechanical ventilation, artificial hydration and nutrition, cardiopulmonary resuscitation, and dialysis machines, which is not what he had in mind for the end of his life. Deciding for a family member without knowing his wishes is very difficult. Before a traumatic event occurs, making your choices known can give your family great comfort.

Cancer specialist Dr. Ranjana Srivastava has worked with terminally ill people for many years. She has recently written a book entitled *Tell Me the Truth: Conversations with My Patients about Life and Death*, in which she questions the way the health system treats people at the end of life. She wrote about one young man with aggressive gastric cancer: "He knows he is dying. We know he is dying. But it is the elephant in the room we are reluctant to acknowledge while we find ourselves distractions that will carry us into another day."

Those distractions consist principally of what Srivastava describes as "an astounding array of tests" that often cause unnecessary suffering, the main aim of which seems to be to allow everybody involved to deny the reality of imminent death.

The young man whose case is described in Srivastava's book did not achieve his desire to spend a few brief hours out of the hospital, to feel fresh air, to play his favorite game with friends, and to go to a picnic or to the movies one last time. Instead, as doctors talked of performing an almost certainly futile liver biopsy, he put an end to the medical interventions by dying in his hospital bed.

Srivastava wrote, "Cancer patients put up with the most and complain the least, endowed with an uncommon wisdom that is a privilege to observe. It is not simply that they see the big picture; if you spend long enough with them, they help you see it, too. What really happens when someone hears the words, 'you have cancer'? What has preceded it and what comes after?" Srivastava writes with great compassion and honesty. As an oncologist she reflects on the very human side of the medical profession, the moral dilemmas, the anxieties, the empathy, and how the best doctors are the ones who keep learning by listening to their patients.

In her work with terminally ill patients, Srivastava has been surprised by how many families, confronted with excruciating decisions about a bewildering array of treatment options, have no idea what the dying person's wishes would be. Srivastava would like to see her medical colleagues become braver about raising the subjects of death and palliative care with patients. Such conversations are not about abandoning hope, she says.

In his book *Death and Dignity: Making Choices and Taking Charge*, professor of medicine and psychiatry Dr. Timothy E. Quill, a former hospice director, states that the care of people with terminal illnesses is among the "highest callings" of physicians. But he argues that medical institutions and the legal system wrongly limit the choices available to terminally ill patients. Quill advances strong arguments for giving the severely ill and those facing lingering deaths options about levels of care as well as the right to a dignified death.

Many cases of suffering patients, and his own experience in assisting a terminally ill woman to die, reinforce his argument that the traditional focus of medicine—to fight death to the end—is not balanced in favor of the patient's comfort care, which, he says, offers the terminally ill the chance to spend their remaining time with less pain and more peace of mind as well as the possibility of dying with more dignity, control, and support.

Quill's book provokes a debate about life, people, and solutions. He is on the side of the dying patient, not the doctor who views death as a defeat to be delayed at any cost, for as long as technology permits.

Quill argues that readers should prepare advance directives to guide their own medical treatments in the event of loss of mental capacity. As in this book, Quill provides samples of living wills and health care directives along with instructions on their use.

Advance planning is absolutely essential before becoming seriously ill, when you will be unable to decide yourself. Your advance care plan should be written down, including the name of the person you choose as your health care proxy. Most common is a spouse or a partner. In some cases a legal guardian with the power of attorney is appointed to make decisions on behalf of the patient. (The legal guardian is a qualified person who is equipped with your written statement of your preferences and can give valid consent for treatment or withholding treatment in the case of an incompetent patient.)

The health plan should include instructions that consent to or refuse specific medical treatments, and a copy of your written plan should be given to the doctors who are caring for you. The plan should be expressed as clearly as possible to enable doctors and care providers to meet your wishes. It should be signed and witnessed.

The expressed wishes of adult patients when they are mentally capable of making decisions are very important. They are usually considered ahead of the wishes of the family. Disagreements between patients and their families may arise in the absence of written advance plans that give direction to the family and the treating team. Families of patients without advance plans might have unrealistic expectations and feelings of guilt and might demand continued treatment without knowing the outcome and without accepting the inevitability of death.

Sometimes the treatment offered might produce some results but still fail to meet your wishes, including independence from life-support machines and surviving after leaving the hospital without being permanently bedridden and becoming a burden on your loved ones.

Remember that legally the advance health directive, which involves withholding or disconnecting life-support systems, is not the same as euthanasia or assisted suicide. In many Western countries, when treatment is withheld or withdrawn and the patient subsequently dies, the law classifies the cause of death as the patient's underlying condition and not the actions of others. Also remember that some religious-oriented hospitals, because of being guided by theological direction and religious dogmas, might create many barriers to your prior expressed wishes. Hospitals that are guided by the dogma of "God gives life and God takes it away" will most likely place God ahead of the patient. Stay clear of these hospitals and any hospices associated with them.

Samples of Advance Health Directives

Below are my personal advance health directive as an atheist and a contrasting one from a fictitious patient named Joseph Christian, a totally committed Catholic. Besides these two versions there are many others that can be written to suit different individuals. The choice is yours. Advance health directives can be as individual as you are.

It is worth remembering that if your circumstances change, you can change your health plan by revoking the old one, including the appointment of a new health care proxy or an enduring guardian if necessary. Irrespective of this the advance health plan should be updated periodically—preferably once a year if you are still competent and especially when the outcome of an illness is predictable, such as with gastric cancer, chronic arthritis, or incurable dementia such as advanced Alzheimer's. This is to ensure that your health care plan is always current. Remember, it is legally binding.

Notes: First, my advance health directive is based on Australian laws and provided as a guide only. It is mostly based on information published by the NSW Department of Health-Australia of 2004 and the third edition of the 2010 booklet entitled "My Health—My Future—My Choice" by Sarah Graham, Anne Hampshire, Elizabeth Hindmarsh, Barbara Squires, and Sharon Wall. (Australian citizens can obtain a booklet by phoning 0423 157 003 or writing to 18/113 Johnston Street, Annandale, NSW 2038.) The instruction on how to prepare the health directive is included in the booklet.

Second, the health directive should be written to suit each individual, relative to his or her circumstances and beliefs. A directive is as individual as the person who makes it. Your directive should coincide not only with your own circumstances but with the laws of the country or the state in which you live. American readers can obtain the information from an organization called Compassion and Choices; in Britain from Dignity in Dying; and in Canada from Choice in Dying. For help, readers in other countries should contact the World Federation of Right to Die Societies or a local medical association. Laws and regulations are different in different countries and states. Advance care plans and directives should be in a format that meets the prevailing legal requirement of the relevant country or state.

Third, the care plan and the directive will only be implemented when the individual becomes mentally incapacitated and incompetent and cannot make his or her own decisions, for example following an accident or after becoming gravely ill. Therefore, the plan should be prepared earlier, when the individual is in good health and of sound mind. To be on the safe side, the plan should be prepared as early as possible before the loss of mental capacity.

The purpose of my advance care plan (advance health directive)

The health directive is to provide hospitals and medical staff with my preferences for life-sustaining treatments, including artificial hydration and nutrition. These preferences will be elicited in the event of specific clinical conditions common at the end of life, including being close to death, stroke, being permanently unconscious, having an advanced progressive illness, being involved in a major accident, and experiencing extraordinary suffering.

In addition, I have appointed my wife, Helen Montan, and my doctor, Dr. J.G.M., to make health care decisions on my behalf if, at a later date, I become incapable due to loss of my mental capacity resulting from illness or accident. I have discussed and made clear my advance plan with my wife and my doctor, and both have copies of my plan, which is entitled "My Health—My Future—My Choice." Close friends and other members of my family are also aware of my preferences.

Note: It is most important that any medical treatment I receive must never cause me to be permanently bedridden or leave me with minimum mobility. I don't want to lose my autonomy, my dignity, and my ability to engage in life's activities. If I become incompetent, I don't want to be a burden on my family or the community.

Hani Montan's Advance Health Directive

Please note I have prepared the following advance care plan, including the advance health directive, when I am in good health and of sound mind. My health directive is to apply in the event of any health circumstances that make my life not worth living and when I lose my mental capacity. This could be after an accident or after becoming gravely ill. For these events I elect my next of kin—my wife, Helen Montan—as my health care proxy, the person responsible for the implementation of my health directive. Helen will give consent to my medical treatment and the termination of medical treatment.

To implement my health care directive, it is necessary to understand my unconventional definition of brain death. Brain death should mean my brain stopped functioning and will never function again despite the fact that my other organs, such as the heart, kidneys, and lungs may still be functioning, as may some of my reflexes. Under these circumstances it is my wish that if I am in coma for more than one day, I must be declared dead and attempts to revive me or to keep me comatose must cease.

The following advance health directive sets out what health care treatment I want. It should be followed when I lose my mental capacity and if I am not able to give my consent to treatment because of injury, cardiac arrest, stroke, brain damage, or any other grave illness including severe to terminal dementia.

The level of functioning I would find unacceptable: If I become terminally ill or permanently demented, or if I enter a persistent vegetative state, I want to die as quickly and as comfortably as possible. If I become unable to read and write, walk, recognize people important to me, communicate, wash myself, dress myself, or control my bladder and bowels, and if I am bedridden or to have a bad general quality of life, or if there are any other conditions associated with permanent mental incapacity, I refuse any and all treatments that would result in prolonging my life.

Under these circumstances I will not accept and specifically refuse artificial hydration and nutrition, cardiopulmonary resuscitation, intensive or active levels of care or palliative care, tube or intravenous feedings, or dialysis and blood transfusions. Furthermore, my wish is to disconnect all life-support systems, and, if possible, my death should be hastened with medicine and sedation.

The level of functioning I would find acceptable: If the prognoses of my illness indicate I will get better and gain my normal functions, and my mobility will not be impeded, I would want only conservative treatment intended to reverse my medical conditions with antibiotics for infection, blood transfusion for anemia, and/or other measures to increase my comfort. The treatment must not include extraordinary invasive treatments such as cardiopulmonary resuscitation, mechanical ventilation, or kidney dialysis, or any other treatment associated with critical and intensive care.

Persons responsible are: (Please note, to protect their privacy, addresses, phone numbers and signatures are not shown. All information is listed in the original document.)

My details:
I, HANI MONTAN, have voluntarily completed this advance health care directive of my own free will, when I was in good health and of sound state of mind on March 4, 2012.

My address:

My phone number:

My signature:

Witness:
I am the witness to this directive.
I, M.N., verify that HANI MONTAN signed this directive on March 4, 2012 of his own free will, without threats or

offered inducement. I am not a relative of the person completing this directive or of the person responsible, and I am not involved in the person's medical treatment.

My address:

My phone number:

My signature:

My general practitioner:
Name: Dr. J.G.M.

Address:

Phone number:

Please note: For illustration, to contrast my advance health plan, I chose a fictitious name—Joseph Christian—to portray the other extreme. Joseph is assumed to be a totally committed religious person who believes his and everyone else's end-of-life suffering is insignificant when compared to the suffering and death of Jesus on the cross.

Joseph Christian's Advance Health Directive

Please note: I have prepared the following advance care plan, including the advance care directive, when I am in good health and of sound mind. The care directive is to apply in the event of any health circumstances that threaten my life. This could be after an accident or after becoming gravely ill and mentally incapacitated. For these events I elect my next of kin—my wife, Heather Christian—as my health care proxy, the person responsible for the implementation of my health directive. Heather will be the person responsible for giving consent for my medical treatment.

To implement my care directive, it is necessary to understand that Heather and I are totally committed Catholics who believe in the sanctity of life, that God gives life and God takes it away, and that God has sovereignty over us. Under these circumstances it is my wish that I should not be declared dead until my last breath and last heartbeat.

The following advance health care directive sets out what health care treatment I want. It should be followed if I am not able to give consent for treatment because of injury, cardiac arrest, stroke, brain damage, or any other grave illness, including severe to terminal dementia.

The level of functioning may be unacceptable but I'm happy to tolerate: Being in constant pain, being in a vegetative state, having a stroke, suffering a cardiac arrest, or being in coma. Under these circumstances, I will accept cardiopulmonary resuscitation, intensive, active levels of care or palliative care, tube or intravenous feedings, and blood transfusions. My wish is not to disconnect any life-support systems, and my death should never be hastened with medicine. In the event of needing palliative care for the rest of my life, I wish to be admitted to a Catholic palliative care center that excludes palliative sedation because I believe suffering is good for the redemption of my soul.

The level of functioning I would find acceptable: If the prognoses of my illness indicates that I will not get better and regain none of my previous functions except for breathing and heartbeat, I should be treated with critical or intensive levels of care for as long as it takes and at all costs. I will want medical staff to try to save my life. I will accept hydration and nutrition, cardiopulmonary resuscitation, kidney dialysis, tube feeding or intravenous feeding, blood transfusions, and palliative care. However, palliative care must not include palliative sedation; I consider that a form of assisted suicide, which is in conflict with my religious beliefs.

Persons responsible are: (Please note, to protect their anonymity, privacy, addresses, phone numbers, and signatures are not shown. All information is listed in the original document.)

My details:

I, JOSEPH CHRISTIAN, have voluntarily completed this advance health care directive of my own free will, when I was in good health and of sound state of mind, on March 4, 2012.

My address:

My phone number:

My signature:

Witness:

I am the witness to this directive.

I, W.C., verify that JOSEPH CHRISTIAN signed this directive on March 4, 2012 of his own free will, without threats or offered inducement. I am not a relative of the person completing this directive or of the person responsible, and I am not involved in the person's medical treatment.

My address:

My phone number:

My signature:

My general practitioner:
Name: Dr. K.L.F.

Address:

Phone number:

Confirming note: Besides the above two contrasting versions of advance health directives, there are many others that can be written to suit different individuals. The choice is yours.

In conclusion it is appropriate to highlight some of the experiences and thoughts expressed by Dr. Timothy E. Quill in his book *Death and Dignity*. The book is about his work as a young resident in the emergency department of Rochester Hospital in New York—in particular one day when three separate cardiac arrest patients came under his care.

The third case is the most moving and relevant to the discussion in this book. Dr. Quill wrote:

> The third cardiac arrest that I treated that day occurred on the surgical floor of the hospital. The patient was an eighty-year-old man who weighed eighty pounds. He was near death from widely metastatic lung cancer, yet was still receiving chemotherapy in a last-ditch effort to prolong his life. This unfortunate

man was literally skin and bones, having lost sixty pounds from the ravages of advanced cancer. His surgeon had strongly recommended and carried out lung surgery in spite of clear evidence that the cancer was already widely spread, and he had continued chemotherapy despite it adverse effects and little evidence that it was helping.

The surgeon adamantly believed that doctors and patients must always fight for life no matter what the burdens or the odds, and he had powerfully and repeatedly admonished his patient not to give up on medical treatment. As we ran into the room to begin cardiopulmonary resuscitation, we encountered a frail, wasted, dying old man. Could we possibly carry out this invasive, often brutal procedure? We didn't know the patient's wishes, but we did know that cardiopulmonary resuscitation is futile when patients are this severely ill. Every instinct in me said no to resuscitation—that our job for such terminally ill person is to comfort and to ease the passage into death.

Unfortunately, the patient's attending surgeon also arrived, and his view was that the fight for this man's life must continue. In the hospital power hierarchy, the attending physician's decision clearly overrides that of the resident (and unfortunately sometimes that of the patient). Delaying cardiopulmonary resuscitation a few moments to clarify and negotiate would have ensured the patient's brain death. So we put a tube down this dying man's throat, and began pressing on his chest, shocking his heart, and giving him medicines. The bones in his chest were so frail that they fractured easily. His heart compressions were accompanied by a sickening crunch of broken ribs. There was no sign that he was responding in spite of repeated electrical shocks, chest compressions, and artificial ventilation, yet the surgeon still did not want to give up. After fifteen agonizing minutes, and no sustained response from the patient, the surgeon wondered out loud if he should surgically open the patient's chest so that he could directly massage the heart. I again told him my belief that further resuscitation was futile and that I was not going to participate anymore. After a difficult exchange, in which my dedication to medicine was challenged, the resuscitation was stopped and the patient pronounced dead.

I left the room profoundly disturbed. I felt that not only had we violated this dying man, but I too had been violated by being forced to act in a way I found both personally and professionally intolerable. How could we repeatedly brutalize this poor man in the name of extending life? Could this be what the Hippocratic Oath intended? Did this man know he was dying, and if so, would he have chosen such an end? How could this attending surgeon, whom I knew from other settings to be a caring, competent individual, not see this man's suffering or the brutality and futility of the attempt at cardiopulmonary resuscitation? Should I have refused to participate from the start? Did I compromise myself and my professional future in the eyes of my superior by openly challenging his orders? The questions flowed fast and furiously. One answer emerged: When I left my residency and became an attending physician, I would do everything in my power to help patients make more informed choices toward the end of their lives, and to avoid futile, invasive medical interventions. I knew then, as I know now, that when someone is dying, alleviating suffering becomes more important than prolonging life.

I left the hospital that day excited about medicine's potential, but disturbed by its capacity to harm by blindly trying to extend life. If as physicians we have a mandate *always* to prolong life, then dying is an affront to our professional mission—something to be fought at all costs. The Hippocratic Oath that we take as physicians cannot be that simple.

Chapter 4

* * *

The Hippocratic Oath

* * *

Euthanasia and assisted suicide are opposed by the majority of the national medical associations in the world and prohibited by the law in most countries. Because of religious influence and control, a change in the legal status of these practices in the Western world would represent a major shift in social values and behavior. For the medical profession to support such a change and subsequently participate in these practices, a fundamental reconsideration of traditional medical ethics and religious influence would be required.

Doctors, other health professionals, academics, interest groups, the media, politicians, and the judiciary are all deeply divided about the advisability of changing the current legal prohibition of euthanasia and assisted suicide. Because of the controversial nature of these practices, their undeniable importance to physicians, and their unpredictable effects on the practice of medicine, these issues must be approached by ridding society of the influence of ultraconservative theologians and the religious-right groups on politicians. These groups are currently in control of the political agendas in some Western countries with their lobbying power and vocal campaigning. They are motivated by their obsession with imposing their non-secular principles on everyone.

Although euthanasia and assisted suicide are not mentioned explicitly in any of the Hippocratic oaths, the current oath has traditionally been interpreted as opposing them. These oaths should be rewritten to coincide with the twenty-first century's prevailing secular attitudes.

An updated oath must ensure patients' autonomy and independence as well as doctors' legal autonomy are protected when it comes to euthanasia and assisted suicide. It is necessary for the updated oath to reflect the secular nature of the silent majority.

The Hippocratic Oath is one of the oldest binding documents in history. The original oath was written back in the fifth century BC and is still held sacred by some medical practitioners. It was about treating the sick to the best of the doctor's ability, preserving patients' privacy, and teaching the secrets of medicine to the next generation.

As can be seen below, the oath has evolved and been amended many times since its invention. The suggested "Medical Oath" below is now ready for debate (free of religious fervor) and adoption to accommodate the questions of euthanasia and assisted suicide, especially in light of the success of euthanasia as practiced in the Netherlands and assisted suicide in Oregon. Terminally ill patients who are in desperate need of termination of their unbearably painful lives deserve humane and serene deaths. It is time to get rid of hypocrisy and introduce uniform laws that avoid the current confusion and clarify the role of doctors and society in the implementation of the practices of euthanasia and assisted suicide. Currently many patients nearing death are abandoned by their doctors on religious and legal grounds. This is the time when patients are in desperate need of their doctors' compassion and assistance to rest in peace.

Euthanasia is the putting to death, by painless method, of a terminally ill or severely debilitated person through the omission (intentionally withholding a life-saving medical procedure, also known as passive euthanasia) or the commission (voluntary active euthanasia) of an act. The reality of modern medicine is that some doctors do practice passive euthanasia. Rare is the doctor who has not, at the request of the patient, the patient's family, or of his or her own accord, decided to discontinue life support. Doctors must, when the death of a patient appears to be inevitable, act so that it occurs with dignity and ensure that the patient obtains the appropriate support and relief.

It is worth noting that Hippocrates, the celebrated Greek physician, was a contemporary of the historian Herodotus. He was born in the island of Cos between 470 and 460 BC and belonged to a family that claimed descent from the mythical Aesculapius, son of Apollo. There was already a medical tradition in Greece before his time, which he inherited through his predecessor, Herodicus; he enlarged his education by extensive travel. He died at Larissa between 380and 360 BC.

The Original Hippocratic Oath

(From Tripod.com)

I swear by Apollo the physician, Aesculapius, and health, and all-heal, and all the gods and goddesses, that, according to my ability and judgement, I will keep this Oath and this stipulation.

To reckon him who taught me this Art equally dear to me as my parents, to share my substance with him, and relieve his necessities if required; to look up his offspring in the same footing as my own brothers, and to teach them this art, if they shall wish to learn it, without fee or stipulation; and that by precept, lecture, and every other mode of instruction, I will impart a knowledge of the Art to my own sons, and those of my teachers, and to disciples bound by a stipulation and oath according the law of medicine, but to none others.

I will follow that system of regimen which, according to my ability and judgment, I consider for the benefit of my patients, and abstain from whatever is deleterious and mischievous. I will give no deadly medicine to anyone if asked, nor suggest any such counsel; and in like manner I will not give a woman a pessary to produce abortion.

With purity and with holiness I will pass my life and practice my Art. I will not cut persons labouring under the stone, but will leave this to be done by men who are practitioners of this work. Into whatever houses I enter, I will go into them for the benefit of the sick, and will abstain from every voluntary act of mischief and corruption; and, further from the seduction of females or males, of freemen and slaves.

Whatever, in connection with my professional practice or not, in connection with it, I see or hear, in the life of men, which ought not to be spoken of abroad, I will not divulge, as reckoning that all such should be kept secret.

While I continue to keep this Oath unviolated, may it be granted to me to enjoy life and the practice of the art, respected by all men, in all times! But should I trespass and violate this Oath, may the reverse be my lot!

The irony is that despite the fact that in this oath doctors swear to give no deadly medicine to anyone if asked and not to suggest any such counsel, in ancient Greece and Rome, terminally ill people were free to ask for a "good death." It was common for doctors, with the consent of the patient, to give a drink called hemlock, a poison extracted from *conium maculatum*, a member of the parsley family. (Hemlock can be a conifer tree or a waterweed).

For over 2,000 years Socrates exemplified the drinking of hemlock as a symbol of rational suicide and freedom of choice. Socrates chose his own death in 329 BC after spending hours discussing with his colleagues whether he should accept the death sentence inflicted by the courts for corrupting the youth of Athens or accept a lonely exile. The choice was not a hasty and hurtful suicide but an accelerated death brought about through thoughtful and rational reasoning.

As for the other matters, medical practice was free and surgical procedures were left to the surgeons. Regarding the anti-abortion question that says "I will not give a woman a pessary to produce abortion," it is now past history, except for in the "Bible Belt" states where religious-right groups are in control of the social and political agendas. All over the world, abortion, including on-demand, is for many reasons now common. Medical associations around the world should follow the same reasoning and principles to accept and advocate the practice of euthanasia and assisted suicide. It is a human rights issue.

Note that in the twelfth century AD, the Catholic Church decreed to ban the use of hemlock on the grounds that a doctor was not meant to play God. The theologians thought a painful death was necessary for the redemption of the soul and the hemlock was against God's intention. This was when the current human misery started—from religious dogma and biblical interpretations by ultraconservative theologians.

Also note that hemlock is the name adopted by the right-to-die movement, a not-for-profit organization named the Hemlock Society, with the motto "good life, good death." Remnants of the Hemlock Society and its offspring, End-of-Life Choices and Compassion in Dying, have merged and are controlled by one new board under the new name Compassion and Choices. Some members of the group were not satisfied with the merger; they broke away to form a new group called Final Exit Network. The group recommends the drug Nembutal, which is commonly used in euthanasia and assisted suicide. It produces the best results and a peaceful death due to its sedative quality. (For more information on Nembutal, Compassion and Choices, and Final Exit Network, see chapter 8.)

Later Version of the Hippocratic Oath

(From Tripod.com)

I swear in the presence of the Almighty and before my family, my teachers and my peers that according to my ability and judgment I will keep this Oath and Stipulation.

[I swear] to reckon all who have taught me this art equally dear to me as my parents and in the same spirit and dedication to impart knowledge of the art of medicine to others. I will continue with diligence to keep abreast of advances in medicine. I will treat without exceptions all who seek my administrations, so long as the treatment of others is not compromised thereby, and I will seek the counsel of particularly skilled physicians where indicated for the benefit of my patient.

I will follow that method of treatment which according to my ability and judgment, I consider for the benefit of my patient and abstain from whatever is harmful or mischievous. I will neither prescribe nor administer a lethal dose of medicine to any patient even if asked nor counsel any such thing. I will perform the utmost respect for every human life from fertilization to natural death and reject abortion that deliberately takes a unique human life.

With purity, holiness, and beneficence I will pass my life and practice my art. Except for the prudent correction of an imminent danger, I will neither treat any patient nor carry out any research on any human being without the valid informed consent of the subject or the appropriate legal protector thereof, understanding that research must have as its purpose the furtherance of the health of that individual. Into whatever patient setting I enter, I will go for the benefit of the sick and will abstain from every voluntary act of mischief or corruption and further from the seduction of any patient.

Whatever in connection with my professional practice or not in connection with it I may see or hear in the lives of my patients which ought not be spoken abroad, I will not divulge, reckoning that all such should be kept secret.

While I continue to keep this Oath unviolated may it be granted to me to enjoy life and the practice of the art and science of medicine with the blessing of the Almighty and respected by my peers and society, but should I trespass and violate this Oath, may the reverse by my lot.

Both oaths are against abortion and assisted suicide. To maintain the religious theme and the Catholic Church's influence, in the later version of the oath Apollo is replaced by the Almighty. However, the main difference in the later version is an item that is in conflict with contemporary medical reality. It reads: "I will treat without exceptions all who seek my administration, so long as the treatment of other is not compromised." The reality now is that hospitals are overstretched, working within budgets and with limited resources including shortages of medical personnel, hospital beds, and emergency beds. Additionally the system is overwhelmed by the aging population. A shortage of hospices and nursing homes aggravates the problem even further, especially for the hospitals' emergency departments. Hospitals are fast becoming glorified nursing homes where treatment of the elderly is a priority.

All these factors make it impossible for doctors not to make exceptions for many patients who end up compromising the treatment of others. Often emergency beds are occupied by patients with no hope of survival whilst other patients who may have better chances to pull through are left waiting. Furthermore, when emergency beds in one hospital are full, patients are ferried around to other hospitals—a process that diminishes their chances of timely treatment or survival.

Neither oath mentions palliative sedation, euthanasia, or assisted suicide. Many doctors consider helping terminally ill and suffering patients to die peacefully to be morally acceptable and believe it should be part of medical treatment despite the fact that it contradicts the part of the oath that states "I will neither prescribe nor administer a lethal dose of medicine to any patient even if asked nor counsel any such thing. I will perform the utmost respect for every human life from fertilization to natural death and reject abortion that deliberately takes a unique human life."

It is obvious that this version of the Hippocratic Oath is too rigid and heavily influenced by outdated religious dogmas. It is in conflict with prevailing social attitudes, and it is well overdue for an update to include freedom of choice as dictated by the human rights principle, especially in relation to abortion and assisted suicide.

The World Medical Association Oath, Based on the Declaration of Geneva

This was adopted by the General Assembly of the World Medical Association, Geneva, Switzerland, in September 1948 and amended in 1966 and 1983.

The original Physician's Oath was as a response to the atrocities and medical crimes committed by the physicians in Nazi Germany.

Specifically the oath requires physicians not to use their medical knowledge contrary to the laws of humanity. It reads:

> I solemnly pledge myself to consecrate my life to the service of humanity.
>
> I will give my teachers the respect and gratitude which is their due.
>
> I will practice my profession with conscience and dignity.
>
> The health of my patient will be my first consideration.
>
> I will respect the secrets which are confided in me, even after the patient has died.
>
> I will maintain by all the means in my power the honor and the noble traditions of the medical profession.
>
> My colleagues will be my brothers.
>
> I will not permit considerations of religion, nationality, race, party politics, or social standing to intervene between my duty and my patient.
>
> I will maintain the utmost respect for human life from its beginning even under threat, and I will not

use my medical knowledge contrary to the laws of humanity.

I make these promises solemnly, freely and upon my honor.

The Amended Declaration of Geneva

I solemnly pledge to consecrate my life to the service of humanity.

I will give to my teachers the respect and gratitude that is their due.

I will practice my profession with conscience and dignity.

The health of my patient will be my first consideration.

I will respect the secrets that are confided in me, even after the patient has died.

I will maintain by all the means in my power the honor and the noble traditions of the medical profession.

My colleagues will be my sisters and brothers.

I will not permit considerations of age, disease or disability, creed, ethnic origin, gender, nationality, political affiliation, race, sexual orientation, social standing, or any other factor to intervene between my duty and my patient.

I will maintain the utmost respect for human life.

I will not use my medical knowledge to violate human rights and civil liberties, even under threat.

I make these promises solemnly, freely and upon my honor.

There is no mention of the almighty God, which is a step toward freeing doctors from religion. Unfortunately, some doctors' judgments are still influenced by their own religious beliefs. The amended declaration has "sisters" added to "brothers" as colleagues, which is also a step forward in acknowledging women doctors.

All the above oaths and declarations don't take into account the growing number of physicians who feel that the oaths are inadequate in addressing the realities of the medical world, which has witnessed huge scientific, economic, political, and social changes including legalized abortion, medical experimentation, organ donation, confused legal responsibilities, euthanasia, and physician-assisted suicide. Many doctors are now raising questions about the oath's relevance. For example, how can doctors keep patients' secrets and privacy with governments, health care organizations, and insurance companies demanding patient information like never before? Furthermore, doctors feel there is no provision for the cultural, secular, and non-secular diversity of different societies.

It is no wonder that many doctors see oath-taking as just a ritual with little value beyond upholding outdated traditions. Its near-meaningless formalities are devoid of any influence on how medicine is truly practiced. There is little that relates to modern doctors and their interactions with their patients. There is nothing that relates to the practices of abortion, euthanasia, and assisted suicide, the demands for which are growing fast.

It is unfortunate that both the World Medical Association Oath and the Amended Declaration of Geneva ignore the fact that modern medicine can cure many illnesses and prolong the lives of patients to unsustainable levels, which often results in prolonging painful deaths. Furthermore, in many cases, they cannot deal with the problem of the aging population or offer a moral solution to end-of-life suffering. The declarations and the oath don't take into consideration the pain and suffering caused by aggressive medical treatment of the dying patient. Generally the declaration and the oath are not in accord with the desire of over seventy percent of people who want to end their lives peacefully and painlessly. It is also against the desire of sixty percent of physicians who favor the legalization of assisted suicide as a humane solution.

This is what probably prompted Dr. Louis Lasagna to produce a modernized version of the oath. His revised oath contrasts sharply with the uninspiring themes of the classical oaths and other declarations. His themes are more in accord with medical practice of the twentieth century by expressing the mission and complexity of the profession, and they offer the appropriate breadth and inspiration for the graduation of new physicians as well as for all of their personal renewal from time to time.

Louis Lasagna's Version of the Hippocratic Oath

Written by Dr. Louis Cesare Lasagna in 1964 when he was the dean of the School of Medicine at Tufts University, this progressive oath was the first to include phrases that indirectly resembling passive euthanasia, assisted suicide, and the impact of patients' conditions on their families and economic stability. Throughout Lasagna's distinguished career he wrote and lectured extensively on a variety of topics. He was well known for his humanity in addressing such controversial topics as birth control, abortion, euthanasia, and medical experimentation on humans. In 1964 he wrote a modernized version of the Hippocratic Oath that emphasized a holistic and compassionate approach to medicine. Today the Lasagna Oath has been adopted by many medical colleges. It reads:

> I swear to fulfill, to the best of my ability and judgment, this covenant:
>
> I will respect the hard-won scientific gains of those physicians in whose steps I walk, and gladly share such knowledge as is mine with those who are to follow.
>
> I will apply, for the benefit of the sick, all measures which are required, avoiding those twin traps of overtreatment and **therapeutic nihilism**. (*see below)
>
> I will remember that there is art to medicine as well as science, and that warmth, sympathy, and understanding may outweigh the surgeon's knife or the chemist's drug.
>
> I will not be ashamed to say "I know not," nor will I fail to call in my colleagues when the skills of another are needed for a patient's recovery.
>
> I will respect the privacy of my patients, for their problems are not disclosed to me that the world may know. Most especially, I must tread with care in matters of life and death. If it is given me to save a life, all thanks. But it may also be within my power to take a life; this awesome responsibility must be

faced with great humbleness and awareness of my own frailty. Above all, I must not play at God.

I will remember that I do not treat a fever chart, a cancerous growth, but a sick human being, whose illness may affect the person's family and economic stability. My responsibility includes these related problems, if I am to care adequately for the sick.

I will prevent disease whenever I can, for prevention is preferable to cure.

I will remember that I remain a member of society, with special obligations to all my fellow human beings, those of sound mind and body as well as the infirm.

If I do not violate this oath, may I enjoy life and art, respected while I live and remembered with affection thereafter. May I always act so as to preserve the finest traditions of my calling and may I long experience the joy of healing those who seek my help.

In this oath, for the first time, humane comfort care versus aggressive invasive treatment is mentioned in the inclusion of the application of warmth, sympathy, and understanding that may outweigh the surgeon's knife or the chemist's drug. There is also the indirect mention of passive euthanasia and assisted suicide in the part that reads:

I will respect the privacy of my patients, for their problems are not disclosed to me that the world may know. Most especially, I must tread with care in matters of life and death. If it is given me to save a life, all thanks. But it may also be within my power to take a life; this awesome responsibility must be faced with great humbleness and awareness of my own frailty. Above all, I must not play at God.

* **Therapeutic nihilism** is a contention that curing people or societies of their ills by treatment is impossible. In medicine it was connected to the ideas that many "cures" do more harm than good and that one should instead encourage the body to heal itself.

Dr. Louis Cesare Lasagna (1923-2003) was an internationally recognized and respected expert in clinical pharmacology. He graduated from Rutgers University in 1943 and earned his medical degree from Columbia University in 1947. After completing a clinical research fellowship in anesthesia at Harvard Medical School, he joined the faculty of Johns Hopkins University in 1954, where he established the first-ever clinical pharmacology department. He taught medicine and pharmacology at Johns Hopkins until 1970, when he accepted the position as the first chairman of the Department of Pharmacology and Toxicology at the University of Rochester, School of Medicine and Dentistry, which he held for the next decade (1970-1980). Early in his fourteen-year career at Rochester, Lasagna founded the Center for the Study of Drug Development. In July 1984 the center moved with Lasagna to Tufts University, where he became dean of the Sackler School of Graduate Biomedical Sciences.

From a historical perspective, some elements of the medical profession are evolving in directions that compromise the original spirit and intent of previous oaths and declarations. Rather than see that happen and see doctors increasingly under pressure to exchange one set of values for another, it is necessary for doctors to change their emphases from the preservation of life to the humane assistance of its end, whether it's naturally occurring or artificially induced. These would be individuals not under any Hippocratic Oath but under a suggested twenty-first century "Medical Oath" (see below) that incorporates the evolving practice of abortion, euthanasia, and assisted suicide.

Societies will always have differences of opinion about the sanctity of human life and freedom of choice. It is time to acknowledge women's right to abortion and individuals' right to self-determination and to choose if they wish to live in pain or die with dignity. Doctors who share these beliefs must be free from religious and traditional legal shackles to act according to their consciences and the appropriately dictated safeguards.

Much of the current debates on abortion, euthanasia, and assisted suicide are driven by an ultraconservative religious consideration versus a mindset that places humankind at the pinnacle of evolution. The debate should be moving toward a more balanced human rights perspective and the need to conserve resources and make radical adjustments to avoid overpopulation and human end-of-life suffering.

Some doctors accept the fact that it's illegal to end the life of a suffering patient but covertly bend the laws. For a peaceful death, for example, they recommend an overdose of morphine and sedatives for unconsciousness, coupled with dehydration.

It is also worth noting that some doctors, on religious or legal grounds, abandon their patients at the critical dying stage. This is when the questions of life and death should be the subject of early, honest discussion between doctor and patient. The patient should be made fully aware if the doctor's dogmatic beliefs are going to impede the continuity care in the final stage of life and at its peaceful end.

The next step for the civilized world will be to become fully secular, with a total separation of state and religion and an adoption of freedom of choice as a guiding principle for human rights, especially by legalizing euthanasia and assisted suicide.

As can be seen from the above versions of the Hippocratic Oath, there is huge gap between the current community attitudes toward euthanasia and assisted suicide and the attitudes of conservative medical associations and the legislators who take their instruction from the vocal, undemocratic, ultraconservative and religious-right groups.

The Medical Oath

To meet present and future community expectation in building a true health care system in a true secular democracy, Dr. Lasagna's version of the Hippocratic Oath should be updated and converted into a general medical oath that reads:

The Medical Oath

I swear to fulfill, to the best of my ability and judgment, this covenant, and solemnly pledge to devote my life to the service of humanity.

I will respect the hard-won scientific gains of those physicians in whose steps I walk and gladly share my knowledge with those who are to follow.

I will apply, for the benefit of the sick, all measures that are required, avoiding those twin traps of overtreatment and therapeutic nihilism.

I will remember that there is art to medicine as well as science, and that warmth, sympathy, and understanding may outweigh the surgeon's knife or the chemist's drug.

I will not permit considerations of age, disease or disability, creed, ethnic origin, gender, nationality, political affiliation, race, sexual orientation, social standing, or any other factor to intervene between my duty and my patient.

I swear to fulfill and never to abandon the terminally ill and nearing-death patients on legal or religious grounds. Furthermore, I will fulfill the nearing-death patient's desire for a peaceful and dignified end of life irrespective of my religious beliefs and in accordance with the law. I will consider as my utmost priorities the autonomy and well-being of the patient who is terminally ill and facing meaningless suffering.

I will never place God ahead of the patient. However, I will inform the patient, well in advance, if my religious beliefs would influence the recommendation or practice of any medical procedure that might be in conflict with the patient's wishes, in order to help him or her choose an alternative physician.

I will remember that even if the laws prohibit me from assisting a patient to end his life when he is in extreme pain and his life has become meaningless, or when he doesn't want to be a burden on his loved ones, I will guide him to the best available information on how to end his life peacefully and with dignity. I will provide patients with the information they need to help them decide on their medical care or termination of their lives and answer their questions to the best of my ability.

I will remember a woman owns her body and has the full right to request an abortion. If it is within my capacity, I will perform the procedure to the best of my ability. If not, or if it is in conflict with my religious beliefs, I will refer her to a physician in the appropriate field of medicine.

I will remember the patients have democratic and human rights to free access to information to help them act upon their freedom of choice.

I must tread with care in matters of life and death. If it is given me to save a life, all thanks. But it may also be within my power to take a life. This awesome responsibility must be faced with great humbleness and awareness of my own frailty.

I will provide appropriate comfort care for the patient, including physical comfort and psychosocial support, even when a cure is no longer possible.

I will respect the right of a competent patient to accept or reject any medical care I recommend.

I will recognize the patients' wishes about the initiation, continuation, or cessation of life-sustaining treatment in accordance with his or her advance health directive or as directed by his or her health care proxy or legal guardian.

I will remember that if the laws allow me to assist a suffering patient to end his life without pain, I will do my utmost to ensure the patient will pass away peacefully. And if the laws allow the practice of euthanasia or assisted suicide, I will do my utmost to follow all the procedures and safeguards laid down in the act and provide all medical comfort care needed to achieve the best possible outcome for the dying patient.

I will respect the privacy of my patients and never disclose their confidential information to anyone, including government agencies and insurance companies.

I will not be ashamed to say "I know not," nor will I fail to call in my colleagues when the skills of another are needed for a patient's recovery.

I will remember that I do not treat a disease but a sick human being whose illness may affect his or her family and economic stability. My responsibility includes these related problems if I am to care adequately for the sick.

I will prevent disease whenever I can, for prevention is preferable to cure.

I will remember that I remain a member of society with special obligations to all my fellow human beings, those of sound mind and body as well as the infirm.

If I do not violate this oath, may I enjoy life and art and be respected while I live and remembered with affection thereafter. May I always act so as to preserve the finest traditions of my calling, and may I long experience the joy of healing those who seek my help.

I make these promises solemnly, freely, and upon my honor.

Note: before the finalization of the above Medical Oath, it should be subjected to a constructive debate that is free from emotive slogans.

Chapter 5

Arguments For and Against Euthanasia

Discussion

Euthanasia and assisted suicide are matters of continuing controversy and hot subjects for debate. Positions range widely, including advocacy for, guarded acceptance of, outright rejection of, or vehement condemnation. Some people equate the acts with murder, genocide, or worse. The pro-life and the religious-right groups, driven by their religious dogmas, are vehemently against them and want these views imposed on others. Fair-minded people are for legalization and consider these options part of medical treatment and an essential part of democracy, human rights, and freedom of choice.

Generally the debate is regarding active, voluntary euthanasia and assisted suicide rather than passive euthanasia because passive euthanasia has been allowed in the majority of Western hospitals without the objection of religious extremists. Even the conservative American Medical Association has endorsed the practice. Above all it is morally accepted by the Catholic Church, as stated in its 2009 directive of the National Conference of Catholic Bishops: "It is not euthanasia to give a dying person sedatives and analgesics for the alleviation of pain, even though they may deprive the patient of use of reason or shorten his life." This directive was issued to justify palliative sedation, which is common in some hospices and not in others that are managed by the Catholic Church.

No matter what it should be valid therefore, if passive euthanasia and palliative sedation are now common and acceptable, active euthanasia and assisted suicide must become legal. The arguments for euthanasia and assisted suicide are simple and valid when assuming that the right to life must include the right to die and the right to life doesn't mean simply to exist without meaning. Existence with pain and a minimum quality of life is meaningless when the process of dying is part of life, and shortening it under certain circumstance is fully justified. Life doesn't mean a subhuman existence. If the dying process is unpleasant, people should have the right to shorten it or end it peacefully, thus reducing the unpleasantness.

Generally people try to make their lives as good as possible; they have the right to try to make their dying as good as possible as well. Additionally, people have obligations to their friends, their families, and the community. Suffering patients feel that to be cared for day in and day out is impinging on the rights of others, which adds to their feelings of guilt and misery.

These obligations, however, don't mean the patient's right to life is prevented. Right to life and freedom of choice are not meant to be trampled on by any consideration. Patients are free to decide for themselves if they want to continue with all possible treatments till the last breath or ask for professional assistance for a serene exit. A suffering patient's request to die is not a request to be killed; it is a request for mercy. Doctor's killing of a patient who doesn't want to die or without the consent of his health care proxy is in violation of the patient's rights and should be treated as homicide. This is sufficient to guard against any misuse of voluntary euthanasia and assisted suicide, as no doctor wishes to be treated as a criminal. This is also to counter the argument that legalizing euthanasia and assisted suicide may increase the risk of patients who want to be killed.

The laws against homicide are universal in all civilized countries of the world. However, as discussed earlier, the practice of passive euthanasia is surrounded by many gray areas and lacks uniformity in its application, especially in the absence of a proper and updated definition of brain death and for its being **involuntary**. Despite this, the religious industry is going along with it, which is in total contradiction of their theological doctrine.

Furthermore, a lot of money is spent on medical facilities and patients who are going to die in few days or weeks and who are desperate for peaceful exits. These patients are occupying emergency and hospital beds that could be used by other patients who have better chances of survival. It is much better to use such resources on those who have fair chances of recovery. Therefore, the question to be asked is: Who do the pro-life and the religious-right groups want to save in these medical facilities? Is it those who are going to die today or tomorrow or those who have fair chances of recovery?

With the aging population and the elderly's frequent visits to the intensive care unit (ICU), hospitals are gradually turning into end-of-life establishments, which will result in a need for new hospitals that can deal with the other general and younger patients. The religious extremists are making fighting death a major priority in the running of the health system. In basing themselves on the speculative dogma that life and death are in the hands of God, they are ignoring the following facts:

First, spending thirty percent of the health budget on prolonging life at all costs and on very expensive, invasive medical procedures is counterproductive. It diverts funding away from medical fields that are beneficial to others, such as palliative care, medical research and education, and so on. Prolonging life at all costs contradicts the religious dogma of "God gives life and God takes it away" because it is an artificial act and doesn't lead to the natural death their invented God has intended.

Second, medicine should never be influenced by religion to adopt as its primary objective the concept of prolonging life by an aggressive approach. Instead it should be guided by the concept of giving patients comfort and reducing suffering.

In their book *Euthanasia and Physician-Assisted Suicide (For and Against)*, authors Gerald Dworkin, R.G. Frey, and Sissela Bok discuss the issues of withholding and withdrawing life-supporting treatment, palliative care, voluntary euthanasia, and physician-assisted suicide, all of which lie at the heart of these complex and controversial problems.

Technological advances in medicine allow doctors to treat patients very effectively. However, this doesn't solve the problem of the frail and the elderly or the patients who are dying from chronic illnesses for which there are no cures yet. The problem is further aggravated by the use of very expensive, life-prolonging technology that allows patient to be kept alive, attached to machines or in comas, for many years. The situation creates ethical, social, clinical, and legal issues for which politicians have yet to come up with satisfactory solutions.

Professors Dworkin and Frey tackle these issues head-on. They argue that physician-assisted suicide is morally permissible and that it ought to be legal for physicians to provide the knowledge or the means, or both, by which a patient can take his or her own life. They propose that autonomy and relief of suffering are essential for helping a dying patient in a painless and dignified way. They argue against any objection to allowing doctors to fulfil their duties in helping patients who are in desperate need of assisted suicide or voluntary euthanasia. They believe, in certain circumstances, that withdrawal of life-support systems, which results in the death of the patient, is morally equivalent to physician-assisted suicide and voluntary euthanasia because there is no moral asymmetry between refusal and withdrawal of treatment and assisted dying.

There are no moral distinctions between switching off a ventilator, prescribing morphine to relieve suffering that hastens death, and providing a pill that will kill a patient. There is no conclusive moral difference between allowing a patient to die by refusing treatment and by giving a pill since these are merely similar ways of achieving the same end.

Furthermore, Dworkin and Frey reject the concern about the slippery slope. They see no chance of the legalization of euthanasia and assisted suicide leading to mass killing, as portrayed by the religious establishment. Dworkin and Frey reject any real moral difference between physician-assisted suicide and voluntary euthanasia since in both cases the doctor and patient act together. The only difference between the two is in who acts last. They suggest that terminally ill, competent patients should not be denied what they choose because of the fear that perhaps more vulnerable and more numerous patients are likely to be euthanized as well. They believe that many safeguards can be used to prevent such a rationalization of killing. They further argue that the burden of proof falls on those who want to overrule a patient's request and deny the patient an assisted suicide to provide evidence that horrible consequences are likely.

On the other hand, in the same book, Sissela Bok argues against legalizing euthanasia and assisted suicide. She disagrees fundamentally with the approach of Dworkin and Frey, who provide a more focused series of arguments dealing mainly with the ethical and moral aspects of these issues. Bok presents more clinical material as well as historical and literary contexts, and discusses previous experiences with physician-assisted suicide and voluntary euthanasia in the Netherlands and assisted suicide in Oregon. She argues that many cases of voluntary euthanasia and physician-assisted

suicide are not reported. Many patients who were comatose or demented and who had never expressed wishes
for voluntary euthanasia or physician-assisted suicide were
terminated.

However, Bok's argument was contradicted by an independent study published in the October 2007 issue of the
Journal of Medical Ethics, which stated that there had been
no negative impact since Oregon's act went into effect. As
for the Netherlands, a BMC Medical Ethics report published
on October 27, 2009 stated: Dutch physicians substantiate
their adherence to the criteria in a variable way with an emphasis on physical symptoms. The information they provide
is in most cases sufficient to enable adequate review. Review
committees' control seems to focus on (unbearable) suffering and on procedural issues. Physicians reported that the
patient's request had been well-considered because the patient was clearheaded.

Furthermore, since 1990, the *Remmelink Reports* (inves-
tigating both reported and unreported voluntary euthanasia
deaths) has documented the impact of the changes to the
law where VE is concerned. The most recent of these was
published in May 2003. To date the reports have revealed the
proportion of deaths as a result of voluntary euthanasia to
be constant. The Dutch consider this type of reporting critical to the ongoing success of their law and helpful in creating
a well-informed debate. In the third of these reports, it was
suggested that this type of ongoing monitoring contributes
to ongoing social acceptance of euthanasia and assisted suicide. The Dutch government believes that transparency has
its benefits.

Opponents of euthanasia and assisted suicide, no matter
what, still see the danger of violating the right to life as so

great that euthanasia and assisted suicide should be banned, even if it means violating the right to die. This is despite the fact that in countries and states where euthanasia and assisted suicide are legalized it has proven otherwise.

Similarly religious leaders' argument against mercy killing could not be sustained. In opposition to euthanasia they use the phrase *mercy killing* with the emphasis on *killing* instead of *mercy* to discredit the concept of euthanasia and assisted suicide. This is in spite of their acceptance of disconnecting life-support systems from near-death patients, which is *involuntary* euthanasia (the patient has no control over the decision). Their contradiction can also be seen in their application of palliative sedation in some of their own hospices, where the use of heavy doses of tranquilizing drugs such as morphine hastens patients' deaths.

Their hypocrisy is further exposed in their tolerance of the horror of suicide by people who are suffering from physical and psychological pain. Because of their deafening silence, suicide is legal all over the world. Despite their obvious hypocrisy, they brand the humane doctors who assist their suffering patients to die serenely as killers.

They should ask themselves: If suicide and passive euthanasia are okay, why is assisted suicide not okay? In all cases they contradict the Christian teachings "life and death are God's business," "we all belong to God," and "God gives life and God takes it away." The religious crusaders' other contradictions can be seen through their argument that induced death is a bad thing; it is the worst possible violation of the wishes of the person who *does not* want to die. They forget that in the case of someone who *does* want to die, this objection is totally invalid.

Certainly the termination of the life of a patient who is in constant pain, has an awful quality of life, and wants to die with dignity, humanely, and peacefully with medical and professional assistance, must be classified as an act of mercy.

It could be further argued that euthanasia and assisted suicide may be necessary where health resources are limited and when patients with better chances of survival cannot receive required treatment because emergency beds are occupied by patients who cannot be cured and have no chances or desires to survive. Assisting such patients to die peacefully will let them meet their desires and free up valuable resources to treat patients who can be cured and survive. This is where advance planning for death, coupled with a proper process and rigorous regulations to prevent abuse, becomes necessary.

In the majority of the Western world's hospitals, euthanasia is happening already with the acceptance of people's advance planning for death and the deliberate disconnection of life-support systems. In the absence of uniform laws, however, doctors are not applying uniform approaches within the same country, and there is no uniform approach within the rest of the civilized world. The application of different moral rules by different moral crusaders prevents gutless politicians from producing an acceptable moral and ethical code that can become the legal basis for the majority of people to follow happily. The modern moral rules and the ethical code in question here are not the same as the ones dictated to the majority by an ultraconservative minority and religious fanatics who wants to take society back to the Middle Ages, when sinners and heretics were burnt alive at the stake.

The ultraconservative minority should understand that among patients who choose euthanasia or assisted suicide are many religious believers who are in good positions to make comparisons between religious dogmas and their own realities. Their pain from illness, their loss of dignity, and the distress caused by their slow and agonizing deaths have made them choose good deaths over religious dogmas. Additionally, these patients are motivated to choose good deaths because of the terrible effects their illnesses have on their family and friends, which outweighs the benefit of following dogmas based on unproven speculation, including "we all belong to God" and "God gives life and God takes it away." In reality we all belong to ourselves and sometimes to each other.

The irony is: The majority of so-called civilized countries have no laws that allow the humane termination of life, yet there are laws that legalize suicide. The European Convention on Human Rights gives a person the right to die, which means suicide is legal. More specifically English law, based on the Suicide Act of 1961, made it legal for people to take their own lives. This indirectly acknowledges that death in certain circumstances is not a bad thing, which means objections to euthanasia and assisted suicide are invalid and should make it easier to meet suffering patients' requests for euthanasia or assisted suicide. Furthermore, the laws legalizing suicide directly invalidate the argument that "death is God's business."

People instinctively don't want to die, and they usually avoid death because they value life. They want to die only when life becomes unbearable and death becomes good for them or at least a better option. Patients requesting euthanasia or assisted suicide most likely have a bad quality of life and a professional predictions that they are nearing death and that medical treatment will no longer help, which makes their predicament worse. Asking for death does not necessarily mean they have nothing to live for, only that they have decided that after a certain point, the pain outweighs the good things they are leaving behind.

The religious argument is the right to life does not include the right to die and a person's life being ended unnaturally means a violation of human rights. A person's life is given to him by God and thus it should be ended at the conclusion of its natural span. The biggest hypocrisy in this argument is that religious leaders are interfering with the natural spans of their own lives by using all methods to prolong them against God's nominated target day. They don't allow God to take them away in a timely manner. They prolong their lives artificially by using medicines, surgeries, organ transplants, blood transfusions, life-support systems, and so on. Their hypocrisy can only escape the indoctrinated and the blinkered believer.

The other religious argument of "society should prevail over the individual" is a relic of communism, wherein individuals existed for society. This doctrine was the main cause of the collapse of communism. Societies promoting conformity over individualism are also destined to collapse. In my earlier book *Thorny Opinion*, I wrote:

> In conformity where individuals exist for the society, the 'go with the group' principle applies, in which individuals follow the same attitude of the group and obey their leader. The individual cannot dispute the group even when he/she thinks that the group is wrong. Worse still, when the group and their leader

have a divine connection, the individual becomes a
walking zombie and victim of mass psychology with
a total loss of their creativity and individuality.

Although conformity on a national level usually results in
social stability, it could also result in a society susceptible
to a totalitarian and oppressive regime, where religion and
the state have total control over every individual. This was
the case during the Middle Ages and in Nazi Germany, and
currently in Saudi Arabia. In a civilized society, social stability
can be easily achieved through a democratic process and
through society actually existing for the individual. In this
scenario the individual is valued as an essential pillar of the
social structure. This social structure allows individuals to
reach their potential, which benefits the whole society.

In cases of health, however, a balance must be found between
who should prevail: society or the individual. In most cases the
whole society is affected, but the individual and his or her immediate family must make the final decision. Furthermore, in a
free society, an individual's liberty is enshrined in the country's
constitution. Accordingly, in a free society where individuals
are encouraged to be independent, they should be given autonomy, the right to self-determination, and the freedom of
choice to live or to die with dignity. Individuals who have led
independent lives will find it demoralizing to be bedridden and
dependent on loved ones to care for them.

Finally, opponents of euthanasia and assisted suicide also
argue that sometimes people make wrong decisions that
are not in their best interests. The answer is: So what? It is
their choice.

Ultimately, if the humane termination of life works in the
best interests of all concerned and violates nobody else's

rights, then it must be morally acceptable. In specific cases euthanasia and assisted suicide promote the best interests of everyone involved and violate no one's rights. Therefore, they must be legalized.

The Slippery Slope Argument

Opponents of assisted suicide assume the word *suicide* implies that the terminally ill are mentally ill, which means a doctor assisting the suicide of a mentally ill patient is guilty of homicide. It is true and justified that it is a crime in most countries to assist a mentally ill patient to die. The prescription of a deadly barbiturate to a mentally ill patient, for example, which when ingested causes death, is considered a crime. But this ignores the fact that the safeguards, where euthanasia and assisted suicide are legalized, clearly state that the patient who is explicitly requesting euthanasia must be of sound mind. In emergency situations, when the patient is unconscious but expressed his wishes earlier when he was of sound mind, the termination of life on compassionate and freedom of choice grounds (as discussed in chapters 1 and 3) is now a common practice and totally justified.

In their attempt to obstruct patients' choices for "good death," ultraconservative theologians, especially Catholics, mix freedom of choice with suicide. One of their arguments is that sixty percent of the patients Jack Kevorkian ("Dr. Death") assisted in committing suicide weren't actually terminally ill. The problem is Dr. Kevorkian, who challenged the medical establishment for publicity, believed that people had the right to commit suicide (which is legal) and the right to receive assistance in doing so.

This happened before Oregon, Washington, and Montana legalized assisted suicide. People, driven by their consciences, had no other option but to turn to anybody operating outside the non-secular laws. With the current humanitarian laws in these states in place, patients don't need to go through all the trouble of seeking help for compassionate and peaceful deaths because more doctors are willing to help, provided they are not inhibited by religious dogmas or prohibition laws. Patients also don't need to go through the trouble of travelling to Mexico to purchase barbiturates or all the way to the Netherlands or Switzerland to seek euthanasia or assisted suicide where they are legalized.

The laws of Oregon, Washington, and Montana give patients total control from the beginning to the end, allowing them to stop the procedure at any time. (For laws and safeguards, see chapter 6.)

The religious industry persistently and emotively uses the term *killing* as a stigma against free-minded doctors who don't want to abandon their patients at the dying stage and who believe in freedom of choice and see the merits of assisted suicide. These doctors refuse to abandon their patients in their dying stage on religious and legal grounds. Patients, their families, and these humane doctors see the termination of life, in certain circumstances, as an act of mercy and a human right. These doctors see their roles as serving humanity the best they can and not to be subservient to religious dogmas. Other doctors who fear the backlash of the religious industry and the ones who follow an outdated Hippocratic Oath or their own religious beliefs try unnecessarily to prolong the lives of terminally ill patients by all possible means. Their actions are not necessarily in the best interests of their patients, their patients' devoted families, or the community.

Opponents of euthanasia also argue that the fear of being a burden is a major risk to the survival of those who are chronically ill. They believe if euthanasia and assisted suicide were lawful, that sense of burden would be greatly increased, for there would be even greater moral pressure to relinquish one's hold on a burdensome life. They also believe allowing a terminally ill person to request euthanasia or assisted suicide makes it less likely that adequate efforts would be made for better provisions or palliative care. Rather than help the patient die, opponents believe, the cause of dignity would be greatly helped if more were done to help people live more fully with the dying process.

These arguments ignore the facts that euthanasia and assisted suicide are not compulsory. They also assume chronically ill patients are stupid and don't know what is good for them, which would somehow result in an avalanche of people rushing to euthanize simply because it is legal. Of course the demand for euthanasia and assisted suicide would increase; it would be natural for people to feel elated when they are empowered and liberated from the nightmare of the religious embargo on the terminally ill. People will be further elated when doctors and medical associations are liberated from the hypocrisy of an outdated Hippocratic Oath and the unreasonable religious control. The religious industry's argument against someone making informed decisions based on individual free will is an insult to people's intelligence and contradicts their own belief that the free will is God-given.

They pontificate about helping people to live more fully with the dying process. How can patients live more fully with the dying process when they are twitching in agony, soiling themselves, rolling in pain, slowly drowning in the fluid from their decaying lungs, and so on? Furthermore, the religious industry assumes these patients will be handsomely rewarded by God in heaven for redeeming their souls. It ignores the fact that religion is about the relationship between people and their gods, and nobody should come between them. If they really want to help the terminally ill to have peaceful deaths, why don't they advocate the incorporation of assisted suicide with palliative care? Instead they limit the dying stage to palliative sedation that leads to prolonged and undignified death.

It is understandable that ultraconservative theologians keep their arguments at the level of the infantile thinking they live with on a day-to-day basis. They include in their anti-euthanasia and assisted suicide campaign false statistics, omissions, fear mongering, and lies, which is not acceptable practice in a secular democracy. It is also understandable that religions are not democratic; instead they are tyrannies working within and exploiting democracies, and to them the ends justify the means.

The ultraconservative theologians and their pro-life followers are experts in the psychology of fear in their endeavor to neutralize public opinion, especially when they sense the religious business is under threat. Usually they target the less enlightened section of the community with their fear campaigns. They purposely mask the fact that euthanasia and assisted suicide are initiated systems that would quite adequately and safely alleviate the suffering of those in need. There is nothing involved that humans cannot handle, just as we have handled other problems faced by our species.

Humanity is now witnessing the practices in some of the states in the US, the Netherlands, and other countries and states, proving that it works well and there is nothing to fear despite religious leaders' constant distortion of the official findings to their advantage. The empty slippery slope argument they put forward ignores the clear evidence showing that countries without lawful euthanasia and assisted suicide laws are illegally killing far more people than countries that have such provisions.

With consistent surveys of over seventy percent in favor of legal euthanasia and assisted suicide, there is no credible reason not to make them legal in all Western secular democracies. This silent majority, if it wants real changes to happen, has no option but to shed its apathy and take action including:

First, weeding out, through the ballot box, all religiously committed, non-secular parliamentarians, including the ones who pretend to be secular but act differently.
Second, rejecting and boycotting any religious establishment that is actively engaged in anti-euthanasia and assisted suicide campaigns, on the basis of being undemocratic and acting against freedom of choice and human rights.
Third, actively campaigning and exerting pressure on hesitant politicians who are accustomed to responding only to loud voices—the only way to wake them up and make them act in favor of the majority.

It is the expectation, in a democratic and secular society where religion and state are separate, that the imposition of religious ideals on everyone is not acceptable. Religious dogmas should not be allowed to control people's lives, and religious leaders should not be allowed to dictate their social and political agendas in a secular country where people are entitled to their beliefs and should have the prerogative to choose the way they want to live and die.

The religious industry, with its slogan of "everyone belongs to God" and their assumption of an afterlife, doesn't leave a chance for nonbelievers to take a rational course of action to suit their individual predicaments. It imposes the irrational dogma of "the next life will be better" on everyone. Religious believers have the right to die the way they wish and should not try to deprive nonbelievers of their human rights and freedom of choice by forcing their views down their throats.

Many people have had personal experiences with parents, relatives, friends, and loved ones suffering unbearable physical pain. The majority of these people believe the constant requests of those persons to be released from their pain should have been honored and respected. They should have had the option available to them as it is elsewhere, in more humane jurisdictions.

The religious industry must not ignore the fact that many humane doctors have moved beyond religious dogmas and the outdated Hippocratic Oath and allow suffering patients to pass away serenely by giving information on drug overdoses, the unspoken system of no resuscitation, and so on.

Finally, the religious industry ignores the fact that euthanasia and assisted suicide, where legalized, are accompanied by a huge number of safeguards to prevent misuse.

The irony is: The religious industry is turning a blind eye and acknowledges that occasional covert assisted suicide and termination of life happen in the majority of Western hospitals and elsewhere. Furthermore, in some countries' religious health codes of ethics, there is a fundamental principle that says, "The treatments may legitimately be forgone, withheld, or withdrawn if they are therapeutically futile, overly burdensome to the patient or not reasonably available without disproportionate hardship to the patient, carers or others."

Doesn't this code of ethics, which is applied in some religious hospitals, contradict the religious dogma of "God may intervene and save the patient"? This is when modern technology can keep comatose patients alive for months or even years longer than God supposedly intends and intervenes. Unfortunately, for these events, religious dogma is suspended; otherwise, religious beliefs and teachings and the hypocritical opposition to freedom of choice are happily imposed on everyone, even in a pluralistic society.

Wouldn't it be better for the ethical code to be administered by professional doctors well trained in the ethics of "to do no harm" rather than dictated to people by hypocritical organizations? Doesn't the religious industry's forcefulness amount to power and control rather than power and influence?

The religious industry seems to be happy to see people dying in pain and discarded in palliative care establishments, given extra doses of morphine that may or may not relieve their pain or keep them unconscious till they die. In the process independent and proud patients find it extremely distressing not only to be in constant pain but to be constantly vomiting or wetting and soiling themselves and knowing they are going to die anyway. They are forced to continue living just to satisfy the pontificating, ultraconservative theologians.

This is not to say that some patients have different tolerances to pain, especially the ones who believe Jesus suffered, and therefore they should also suffer. For them, despite the limitation of palliative care and being burdens on family and community, facing illness and disability takes courage, and they do not need euthanasia advocates to tell them they are lacking dignity and have such a poor quality of life that their lives are not worth living. These patients ought to be congratulated for their resilience, and their rights must be respected by all. It is their choice to live till the last breath if they wish, and good luck to them. They are free to suffer as much as they want, be burdens on others as much as they like, and waste as many resources as they want. It is their democratic right and must not be subjected to ideological contempt.

Some people who are blindly committed to religion never blame God for their predicaments; instead they blame themselves, believing they are being punished for their sins. Because God is perfect, nobody is allowed to blame anything on him. These same people, driven by their consciences or by the religious industry, want to impose their religious dogmas on everyone else, especially on clear-thinking citizens and nonbelievers.

Clear-thinking citizens, for example, don't accept the religious definition of death, which is "when the soul leaves the body," because such a definition cannot be sustained on scientific grounds. It is a metaphysical philosophy based on conjecture rather than logic. Clear-thinking citizens also see the irony in the attitude of advocates of the doctrine "God gives life and God takes it away" when they don't allow God to take them in a natural and timely manner. (For discussion of the soul, please refer back to chapter 2.)

The point here, however, is the maintenance of the rights and freedom of choice of others who don't believe in biblical fairy tales, don't have the same tolerance to severe and chronic pain, and don't want to put their loved ones through their agony. These people must also have their human and democratic rights respected and must be allowed to pass away peacefully if they so choose.

The question should be asked: What can religions do for dying patients with severely diminished quality of life and total loss of dignity while their spouses and children observe their daily physical decline, pain, vomiting, and incontinence?

Another irony is: The religious industry knows civilized countries will not allow termination-of-life laws to go beyond the desperate need of a dying patient and the freedom-of-choice principles. However, some civilized countries in NATO, including the United States, as well as Israel display brutality in the killing of many innocent civilians, including women and children. The termination of life using drones, rockets, gunships, and so on has happened or is happening in Lebanon, Iraq, Libya, Afghanistan, Pakistan, Yemen, and Palestine and will happen later in Iran. Not raising an eyebrow at all these atrocities exposes the hypocrisy of the ultraconservative theologians and the followers of the pro-life and right-to-life movements. However, their silence could be because the extermination of people of other faiths is fully justified. The Old Testament endorses the concept of a jealous God and the killing of anybody who incites us to worship another god.

It is interesting to observe that the religious industry, using a funny argument against euthanasia and assisted suicide,

states "Jesus' crucifixion was a form of state-assisted suicide." It is one of their methods of scaring the hell out of
naïve believers.

Another irony is: What can religion do for the people
of Africa, who are dying of hunger and treatable diseases
while the religious industry is fighting for power and control?

The ultraconservative theologians are even against the
use of condoms in poor Africa, which are essential for the
control of HIV and the birth rate. (In March 2009 Pope
Benedict XVI, during his visit to Cameroon on his first trip
to Africa as pontiff, denounced condom use on the AIDS-
ravaged continent, saying there were better ways to combat
the disease. Distribution of condoms aggravates the problem, he said.)

France's education minister, Xavier Darcos (a Catholic),
has condemned the Pope's comments against the use of
condoms as "criminal." In addition many protests against the
pontiff have been held.

The French minister said, "To go to Africa and tell people
they shouldn't use condoms is criminal." He added, "I think
the Pope's comments were a bit distorted but, all the same,
to not encourage using condoms in developing countries is
extremely dangerous."

Overpopulation in an unsustainable environment is a
major cause of environmental destruction, starvation, and
high death rates. The Pope thinks the use of condoms is in
conflict with Christian teachings. Yet the condom had not
been invented at the onset of Christianity, and Jesus didn't
know about it. All people knew at that time was the fairy
tale of Adam and Eve who were ordered by God to "go
forth and multiply." Apparently, by omission, God forgot to
tell them that occasional use of a condom is okay.

Another irony is: The rest of the religious slippery slope argument against euthanasia and assisted suicide is that once a moral precept is breached, a psychological and logical process is set in motion and overwhelms its own justification. This argument may be valid because it is based on the experience of priests' sexual abuse of children as a result of breaching the moral code, which caused their psychological and logical process to become overwhelmed in justification of their actions. (For more detail of the sexual abuse of children, see chapter 6 of my earlier book, *Israel vs. America vs. the World*).

The world is not about to believe these religious merchants, as they were and will always be the leaders of the slippery slope and the masters of covering up massive lies to avoid the legal system. As a consolation, however, they offered and will continue to offer sexual abuse victims and the rest of the world continuous qualified apologies and occasional compensations.

Religion leads to the slippery slope, not the people who want to die peacefully. Throughout history most wars and genocides have been carried out in the name of God and religion.

In the final analysis, the debate over end-of-life choices should not be about religion. It should be about the process of choices for those who fear allowing patients to choose death as a slippery slope and the others who believe it is their human and democratic right to be given end-of-life choices. In this instance human and democratic rights are real, but the slippery slope is a supposition. The Netherlands and Oregon have proven the slippery slope supposition is without foundation and, at best, is an extreme exaggeration by extremist theologians.

In conclusion, the opponents of euthanasia and assisted suicide argue their legalization may lead to possible misuse by doctors when the life of a patient is placed in their hands:

- <u>First</u>, historically, patients have always placed their well-being in the hands of their trusted doctors, and in critical cases second opinions are sought.
- <u>Second</u>, if the safeguards in the euthanasia and assisted suicide legislations are not sufficient, it is the government's responsibility to introduce additional or separate legislation to ensure against any possible abuse by doctors. One of these safeguards can be establishing a quasi-judicial authority with proper knowledge of medicine to oversee the administration of the law. This group can also include a legal expert. This specialists' group should be free from religious prejudice and political interference and have one objective: to ensure the strict implementation of euthanasia and assisted suicide laws. The top priority of the group would be to have regard for patients' rights and their dignity.

Religious Dogmas

The ultraconservative theologians maintain that dying by way of an act of another person is against the sanctity of human life—that the life God has bestowed on people can never be sacrificed for the sake of the good of self-determination. When the prevailing tendency is to value life only to the extent that it brings pleasure and well-being, suffering seems like an unbearable setback, something from which one must be freed at all costs. Death is considered senseless if it suddenly interrupts a life still open to a future of new and interesting experiences.

The decision to request to end one's life by means of an active intervention by another person rests on a misconception that a human life can be not worth living. This contravenes the commandment of God: "Thou shalt not kill."

In the "Gospel of Life" (n. 39), Pope John Paul II explained:

> We do not have absolute dominion over the gift of life: the time and circumstances of death are not ours to choose, for ourselves or for others. This means that euthanasia is never an acceptable response to human suffering. Man's life comes from God; it is his gift, his image and imprint, a sharing in his breath of life. God therefore is the sole Lord of this life; man cannot do with it as he wills. If it is true that human life is in the hands of God, it is no less true that these are loving hands, like those of a mother who nurtures and takes care of her child. Even though we may not fully understand why God permits suffering, we can be certain that He will never abandon us.

All this is nicely and tenderly expressed for the religious idealists who are fully committed to the theological interpretation of Christian teachings, especially the ones who wish for and accept all the suffering they can endure and live happily till their last breaths. The majority, however, deserve to be treated as equal and allowed to die with dignity, especially if they cannot endure the suffering and if they don't believe in religious mumbo jumbo, as expressed above.

The irony is: The religious teaching is about convincing people to fear God and to believe in the afterlife and final judgment, which will result in going to heaven or hell. Yet the religious industry wants people to be judged now and not wait for God's final judgment.

The other irony is: For centuries religious leaders controlled the moral code while instilling divisiveness and hatred between various sects to bolster their position and secure their brand of religion as a competitive commercial enterprise. The subjectivity of religion and the fragmentation it has created manifest themselves in the teaching of the Old Testament "not to worship another god and to kill anybody who incites you to do so, because our God is jealous." Throughout history religious wars killed millions of innocent people in contradiction to the slogan of "thou shalt not kill."

Furthermore, many more people will be killed as a consequence of the rise of the Dominionists, also known as the Christian Reconstructionists, who fanatically believe in the concept that "Christians are Biblically mandated to [occupy] all secular institutions as the central unifying ideology for the Christian right." The central unifying ideology of their social movement is to take dominion over the secular institutions of the United States. Their survival largely depends on entangling religion with politics. To achieve their objectives, they have decided to gain political power through the warmongering Republican Party, which they were able to convert into a party of theocracy where religion and politics have become inseparable. Hence it has become a nonsecular party driven by the Tea Party.

The Dominionists claim that Christian men with specific theological beliefs are ordained by God to run society. Christians and others who do not accept their theological beliefs would be second-class citizens. Their fundamental-ist belief is in the apocalyptic end of times and the return of Christ theology. The second coming of Christ and cata-strophic end-time event has destructive consequences. The clash of Christianity and secular governments as part of God's intervention to save mankind from self-destruction and the establishment of God's government by ending man's self-rule can lead the world into a catastrophe.

The ridiculous aspect of these beliefs is the killing of billions of people to save them from self-destruction. This doesn't add up, especially when considering that humans have, over millennia, proven to be rational thinkers equipped with the natural instincts of survival and self-preservation. Furthermore, this ideology is totally against the civilized and constitutional secular system of government, where religion and state are separated. This brand of religion, unfortunately, is spreading to other countries, especially to the Anglo-Saxon countries, which is causing the current clash of civilizations.

Religious interpretations

Ultraconservative theologians say that voluntary euthanasia and assisted suicide contravene the sanctity of life. More-moderate religious leaders say the opposite. According to Reverend Trevor Bensch, cofounder of Christians Supporting Choice for Voluntary Euthanasia, the term *sanctity of life* appears nowhere in the Bible. Interpreting selected passages of the Bible to mean so is a personal matter. One could equally interpret other passages of the Bible to authorize or justify selling daughters into slavery or killing people who tell others to believe in a different god. Voluntary euthanasia and assisted suicide don't require anyone to accept them, and anyone is free to die in accordance with his or her personal beliefs and values.

According to Ian Wood, a spokesman for the same group, many Christians support euthanasia. He says:

> Most of the opposition is from church hierarchies. We have members who are Anglican, Baptists, Catholic, and Church of Christ. We have even got Jehovah Witness members. ... The message of Jesus is love and compassion and that is what should be involved in the discussion about the legislation of voluntary euthanasia. It is about people in the final phase of their terminal illness, or people whose condition or illness is so bad that they are permanently unconscious or their quality of life is so irreversibly impaired that they just can't go on any longer.

Furthermore, in an excerpt from a paper published in the *Monash Bioethics Review* (Vol. 16 No. 2, April 1997), Rev. Dr. Andrew Dutney wrote:

> Even among the experts and authorities, there is a diversity of opinion. Catholicism has an official position of unqualified opposition to any form of euthanasia and according to the catechism, intentional euthanasia, whatever its form or motives, is murder. It is gravely contrary to the dignity of the human person and the respect due to the living God, his Creator. But there are Catholic voices expressing disagreement with that position.

Many Christians take a position of supporting voluntary euthanasia and assisted suicide on the basis of God having created human beings to make their own decisions and accept responsibility for themselves and their neighbors. There is nothing faithful about relinquishing that responsibility in the face of the power of nature or history. According to Australian philosopher Max Charlesworth, "It's not playing God to seek freely to control the direction of my life, and it's not playing God to seek freely to control the mode of my dying. For a Christian, God is not honored by a person (made in the image of God) abdicating his/her autonomy and freedom of will and passively submitting to fate."

Hans Kung, a well-known moderate Catholic theologian, has taken a similar position. He said:

> God, who has given men and women freedom and responsibility for their lives, has also left to dying people the responsibility for making a conscientious decision about the manner and time of their deaths. This is a responsibility which neither the state, nor the church, neither a theologian, nor a doctor can take away…
>
> …Precisely because I am convinced that death is not the end of everything, I am not so concerned about an endless prolongation of my life—certainly not under conditions that are no longer compatible with human dignity.

Kung's views are in conflict with the views of ultraconservatives theologians who think suffering is good for the redemption of the soul.

Similar views have been expressed by Protestant Christians such as Kenneth Ralph, a Uniting Church minister who has argued that "self-determination is central to what it means to be a human being, or a person." The minister resists arbitrary removal of the responsibility of self-determination in the manner of one's death. His views summarize a characteristic emphasis on the human person as it has been stated in twentieth-century Western theology. He said:

> The paramount is: the person was given by God and was central to the ministry and teachings of Jesus. The interests of the individual therefore have priority over any social, political, or religious project to which he or she might be conscripted. In particular, there is no religious value in requiring extreme and hopeless suffering of individuals against their will. Indeed, such use of persons defaces the image of God in them and is to that extent irreligious.

People have made that judgment about themselves and about others for centuries, many choosing to take their own lives or forego treatment. Today, with advances in medical technology, the possibility exists for others to assist people to end their lives relatively painlessly. Euthanasia and assisted suicide, however, must be distinguished from the decision to forego so-called aggressive medical treatment.

As it stands the opponents of religious dogma believe aggressive medical treatment to prolong the life of a dying patient by a few more days or weeks doesn't correspond to the real situation of the patient, either because it is disproportionate to any expected results or because it imposes an excessive burden on the patient and his or her family. In such situations, when death is clearly imminent and inevitable, one can in good conscience refuse forms of treatment or request termination of life with assistance from qualified medical practitioners. This has nothing to do with neither the sanctity of life nor the love of God, who, in the religious leaders' opinions, has created life and controls everything from somewhere in the sky.

Some religious leaders are interested in patients' souls and totally ignore the patients' physical conditions and dignity. Fighting for life at any cost maybe acceptable to totally devoted Christians so long as it is the result of an informed decision-making process in which the patient is not only involved but is the ultimate decision maker. Furthermore, religious and nonreligious people must be made aware of the rules and given the control over their end-of-life choices.

Some people believe in creationism and that the world is designed by God. At the same time, they accept human autonomy. Some others take their beliefs a step further; thinking only the creator who bestows the gift of life may take away life, even when it has become a burden rather than a blessing. Other people believe the sanctity of life should be extended to include all animals because they are also created by God. This contradicts the attitude of some hypocritical religious leaders who raise no objection to animal euthanasia or the killing of animals for sport or human consumption.

Creationism and attitude are in the eye of beholder. People who believe in any form of metaphysics or fairy tales as substitutes for science are entitled to their beliefs and can act accordingly. Some people may believe our fragmented and messy world could only have been designed by a committee rather than by a single creator. It could be the same committee that intended to design a horse but ended up with a camel.

Equally, however, there are people who believe in science and the concept of evolution. These people are also entitled to their beliefs and should be given their human rights and freedom of choice.

It is worth highlighting Derek Humphry's comments regarding the attitude of the Catholic Church toward euthanasia and assisted suicide. During an interview in 1995, Anthony Qaiyum asked: "I understand that you've had trouble with religious groups. Which ones have been your biggest opponents?"

Humphry replied, "The Roman Catholic Church. It's a dedicated opponent."

Then Qaiyum asked, "If you don't mind my asking, would you describe yourself as a religious person?"

Humphry replied, "No, I'm an atheist."

According to British scientist Stephen Hawking, God no longer has any place in theories on the creation of the universe due to a series of developments in physics. In his book *The Grand Design*, Hawking wrote that the Big Bang was merely the consequence of the law of gravity. "Because there is a law such as gravity, the universe can and will create itself from nothing. Spontaneous creation is the reason there is something rather than nothing, why the universe exists, why we exist." He added, "It is not necessary to invoke God to light the blue touch paper and set the universe going."

Although in his earlier book *A Brief History of Time*, Hawking had suggested the idea of God or a divine being was not necessarily incompatible with a scientific understanding of the universe, now he cites the 1992 discovery of a planet orbiting a star outside the solar system as a turning point against Isaac Newton's belief that the universe could not have arisen out of chaos. "That makes the coincidences of the planetary conditions—the single sun, the lucky combination of earth-sun distance and solar mass—far less remarkable and far less compelling as evidence that the earth was carefully designed just to please us human beings," he wrote.

In a recent interview, Hawking said, "You cannot argue against faith. It's a baseless belief, impossible to disprove. What I would like to see is someone to explain the persistence of religion and its purpose in the evolutionary cycle."

Twisted logic

Religious leaders defy logic in the way they blame atheists for global warming. Pope Benedict XVI claimed in a recent speech that atheists are responsible for the destruction of the environment. The claim is a puzzling attack on atheism that frankly makes little sense. What about the Christian Dominionists who subscribe to the idea that "ours is the earth" with the earth, in their interpretation, being merely a temporary waystation on the road to eternal life? The earth was put here by the Lord for his people to subdue and to use for profitable purposes on their way to the hereafter. For those of the Judeo-Christian tradition, the earth is, for all intents and purposes, disposable, as it is nothing but a waiting room for eternity. As such it can be plundered in any fashion. After all, the earth as a temporary and transient thing and is of no consequence when compared to the promise of eternity.

The creationists blame the atheists to cover up the main causes of environmental destruction, which is the over-breeding they advocate to bolster their power through a larger constituency. These are the same people who campaign against birth control and abortions. They cover up the fact that the more the world population increases, the bigger its impact on the environment will be. This is the consequence of the religious dogma "go forth and multiply." The earth's population now stands at an unsustainable seven billion and is rapidly increasing. Yet creationists ignore the simple fact that interfering with the carbon and nitrogen cycles has had a devastating effect on the planet, and soon, when the world population reaches ten billion, the effect will be more catastrophic.

Furthermore, Christian and Muslim competition to increase the populations of their constituencies has a major impact on the environment and global warming. Catholics and Muslims, by believing strength is in numbers, are among the causes of world population growth. Their numbers are currently standing at 1.3 billion each, which is in balance and probably insufficient to restart the crusade or spiritual warfare.

The other aspect of the Pope's speech was his assumption that because atheists marginalize and deny the existence of God, the world is being punished with global warming.

- First, God (if there is one) must be smart enough and have the capacity to punish nonbelievers and can easily spare the others, especially the totally devoted Catholics. Punishing everyone, including the religiously blinkered, for the sins of atheists and people of other faiths is illogical.
- Second, if the Pope wants to follow his own logic, he should be saying God is punishing the world for the sins of his pedophile priests instead of arguing that

the good of the universal church should be considered before punishing the priests or handing them over to police. This is what he did in 1985, in his capacity as head of the Congregation for the Doctrine of the Faith, when he signed a letter in the case of an American priest who committed sex offenses against two boys. It is all part of the practice of covering up throughout the history of the church.

In September 2011 the Survivors Network of Those Abused by Priests (SNAP) filed a complaint calling on the International Criminal Court (ICC) to take action and prosecute Pope **Benedict XVI** for direct and superior responsibility for the rapes and other sexual abuses committed by priests around the world. The US-based victims' network submitted more than 20,000 pages of supporting materials including reports, policy papers, and evidence of the crimes Catholic clergy committed against children and vulnerable adults. Crimes against tens of thousands of victims, most of them children, are being covered up by officials at the highest level of the Vatican.

The cover-ups and subsequent scandals are essential parts of Church history, as demonstrated by a recent revelation in the Australian parliament regarding allegations that over forty years ago a priest raped an archbishop. It was the case of Monsignor Ian Dempsey, a parish priest in the Adelaide suburb of Brighton, South Australia, who allegedly raped the archbishop of the Traditional Anglican Communion, John Hepworth. The church leadership has failed to make appropriate inquiries into this matter and has failed to stand this priest down as a matter of course while inquiries take place. Hepworth has said he was repeatedly raped by three priests over a twelve-year period while training in a Catholic seminary when he was fifteen years old. The matter now is in the hand of South Australian police.

The Catholic Church has a history of hiding crimes behind Canon privilege. They have been looking into this matter for four years and would have continued to look into it for many more years if it hadn't been revealed under privilege in parliament.

The Catholic Church is one of the most evil empires; it has a history of supporting and protecting pedophiles. Yet it blames atheists for global warming, when atheists have much higher moral standards than any of its clergy, including its leaders. Atheists and agnostics, being more open-minded, avoid religious subjectivity and its conflict creation, which causes destruction and death in the name of religion. Atheists and agnostics are better equipped to pass on to the next generation their more realistic, flexible, logical, and objective values without being dogmatic. Atheists and agnostics will never contemplate what the religious leaders did during the sixteenth century when they were engaged in the grotesque sale of indulgences to sinners. This was when the popes allowed a system to flourish whereby ordinary believers could pay the church to be absolved from their sins.

For how long can humanity tolerate the Church's barking? Humanity has moved on while the Church peddles out-of-date dogmas. The world is living by an old Arab adage: "The dogs may bark, but the caravan moves on."

Chapter 6

Laws and Safeguards

In this chapter we'll look at the laws governing euthanasia and assisted suicide in countries and states where they are legalized and practiced. Oregon, Washington, Montana, the Netherlands, Belgium, and Luxembourg are the only jurisdictions in the world where laws specifically permit euthanasia or assisted suicide.

In the US, the states of Oregon and Washington passed laws legalizing the practice of assisted suicide, and Montana's Supreme Court determined assisted suicide is a medical treatment. In Europe, the Netherlands, Belgium, and Luxembourg permit both euthanasia and assisted suicide.

Although euthanasia and assisted suicide are illegal in Switzerland, assisted suicide is penalized only if it is carried out "from selfish motives." It is punishable only if the motive is bad; otherwise, if it is altruistic, the practice condoned. In most cases the permissibility of altruistic assisted suicide cannot be overridden by a duty to save life. Article 115 of the Swiss penal code does not require the involvement of a physician nor that the patient be terminally ill. It only requires that the motive be unselfish. Swiss law does not recognize the concept of euthanasia. "Murder upon request by the victim" (article 114 of the Swiss penal code) is considered less severe than murder without the victim's request, but it remains illegal.

Following a proposal to the Swiss parliament to decriminalize euthanasia in 1997, the federal government commissioned a working group that included specialists in law, medicine, and ethics to examine the issue. This group recommended euthanasia remains illegal. Most of the group, however, proposed decriminalizing cases in which a judge was satisfied that euthanasia followed the insistent request of a competent, incurable, and terminally ill patient in unbearable and intractable suffering. A doctor can provide a patient who wants to die lethal medication that the patient has to take by himself or herself.

The debate in Switzerland is still raging, and most likely it will end up in legalization. (For more information, see below, under the subheading "Switzerland's Euthanasia Laws.")

In 2002 Luxembourg, under strict conditions, became the third European country to legalize euthanasia and assisted suicide after the Netherlands and Belgium. A law published in the official register said doctors who carry out euthanasia and assisted suicides will not face "penal sanctions" or civil suits for damages and interest.

The law was the source of great controversy in the tiny country where the head of state—Grand Duke Henri, a devout Catholic—refused to sign off on the bill, triggering a constitutional crisis. To get around his refusal and avoid such problems in the future, Luxembourg's parliament voted for legislation to give the monarch a purely ceremonial role.

In America the states of Oregon (see below), Washington (similar to Oregon), and Montana allow assisted suicide based on "death with dignity" laws. According to both Oregon's and Washington's death with dignity acts, physicians are allowed to write prescriptions for lethal doses of drugs for terminally ill patients who have less than six months to live. "They don't want to die—they're choosing to end suffering that cannot be relieved and suffering that they are experiencing that is worse than death." Under the legislation any patient seeking a prescription for lethal drugs must be eighteen years old and a permanent resident of the state.

In Montana the court recently ruled terminally ill patients have the right to seek physician-assisted suicide.

The US Supreme Court allows for "aided dying" rather than euthanasia or assisted suicide According to the Washington branch of the Compassion and Choices advocacy group, "aided dying" is neither euthanasia nor assisted suicide. It's not euthanasia because that implies action by a physician to end a patient's life. It's not assisted suicide because people who choose aid in dying are not choosing to end their lives.

In Washington, to obtain a prescription, a patient would need to make two oral requests followed by a written request witnessed by two people who are not related or connected to the individual. Two doctors must also affirm the patient has six months or fewer to live.

Physicians who object to the legislation have the right to decline a request for a lethal prescription and are also not allowed to administer the fatal drugs. Under the law a patient has to self-administer the medication. The laws do not allow doctors to coerce or use undue influence to obtain a request for assisted suicide. Furthermore, anyone who has an objection of conscience may choose not to participate.

In the above progressive countries and states, where individuality, personal liberty, and democratic rights are the anchors of the civil structure, the question of euthanasia and assisted suicide are well behind them. They implemented their euthanasia and assisted-suicide laws successfully and proved the religious scare tactics used against them were totally baseless.

In other countries there is always a debate about what should prevail: the society or the individual. Mostly, in the cases of health concerns, the laws bend toward society's prevailing over the individual. These laws, however, don't take into consideration how the affected individuals and their families, who are impacted by religious considerations, affect the whole society. Individual liberty is the hallmark of any free society. Therefore, consideration should always be given to the rights that accrue for the individuals in such cases.

In some countries, like India, interpretation of the law is very confusing. In one part of the country the laws imply the right to life includes the right to die. The explanation is that the right to die is not unnatural; it is just uncommon and abnormal. Yet, in other parts of India, the interpretation of the law is that the right to life guaranteed by the country's constitution does not include the right to die. The explanation is that the constitution only guarantees the right to life and personal liberty, and in no case can the right to die be included in it. This is the unfortunate situation that patients who are in desperate need of help to end their suffering and maintain their dignity are in.

This emphasizes the argument of supporters of euthanasia and assisted suicide that when patients suffering from terminal diseases can't even take care of themselves, how can they have dignified lives? In that case it would be better if the patients were allowed to end their lives, as other parts of the constitution speak about how a person has a right to a dignified life, which also must include the right to die with dignity. Unfortunately, this is when the reactionary religious dogma "we all belong to God" triumphs over human rights and freedom of choice and places society ahead of individuals and their families. It contradicts the reality of the nonreligious people who believe we all belong to ourselves.

It also contradicts the laws that permit suicide, which is by its very nature an act of self-killing or self-destruction, an act of terminating one's own life without the aid or assistance of any other human agency. Euthanasia and assisted suicide, on the other hand, mean and imply the intervention of other human agencies to end life. Mercy killing thus is not suicide, and an attempt at mercy killing is not covered by the laws of many countries. The two concepts are both factually and legally distinct.

Unfortunately, euthanasia as a mercy killing is considered homicide in semi-secular and non-secular countries no matter the circumstances in which it is implemented. In these countries the pressure brought to bear on politicians by the vocal religious industry is the main obstacle preventing a proper and unemotional debate on the subject from taking place.

The Netherlands' Euthanasia Legislation

The Supreme Court of the Netherlands allows euthanasia and assisted suicide. According to the nation's penal code, killing a person at his request is punishable with twelve years of imprisonment or a fine, and assisting a person to commit suicide is punishable with three years of imprisonment or a fine. But the law provides a defense of necessity to the offenses of voluntary euthanasia and assisted suicide. This defense is twofold, encompassing psychological compulsion and cases of emergency. The criteria laid down by the courts to determine whether the defense of necessity applies in a given case of euthanasia are summarized as follows:

The request for euthanasia must come only from the patient and must be entirely free and voluntary.

The patient's request must be well considered, durable, and persistent.

The patient must be experiencing intolerable (not necessarily physical) suffering, with no prospect of improvement.

Euthanasia must be the last resort. Other alternatives to alleviate the patient's situation must be considered and found wanting.

Euthanasia must be performed by a physician.

The physician must consult with an independent physician colleague who has experience in this field.

Following these judicial guidelines, a bill was passed by the Upper House of the Netherlands Parliament on April 10, 2001 legalizing the practices. The legislation determined the termination of life on request and assistance with suicide would not be treated as a criminal offenses if carried out by physicians and if certain criteria of due care are fulfilled. The legislation allows a doctor to end the life of a patient whose suffering is "intolerable."

Under the legislation a physician who terminates a life on request or assists with a suicide has to comply with two conditions to be exempt from criminal liability:

<u>First</u>, he or she must practice the due care criteria.

<u>Second</u>, he or she must report the cause of death to the municipal coroner.

It should be noted that the incorporation of provisions on exemption from punishment in Articles 293 and 294 of the Netherlands Criminal Code does not decriminalise other forms of termination of life or assistance with suicide. Additionally, under the legislation, patients do not have a right to demand termination of life or assistance with suicide, nor must a physician agree to such a request.

Due diligence: The law allows a medical review board to suspend prosecution and obtain exemption from criminal liability for doctors who perform euthanasia or assisted suicide. To obtain exemption from criminal liability, the doctor must adhere to the following conditions:

The patient has made a voluntary, well-considered request persistently over time, without the influence of others and free from psychological illness or drugs.

The patient's suffering is unbearable, and there is no prospect of improvement.

The doctor has informed the patient about his or her condition, prospects, and options.

The doctor has come to the conclusion, together with the patient, that there is no reasonable alternative in light of the patient's situation.

The doctor has consulted at least one other independent doctor, who must have seen the patient and given a written opinion on the due care criteria referred to above.

The doctor has terminated the patient's life or provided assistance with suicide with due medical care and attention, in which case the doctor must be present.

The patient was at least twelve years old. (Patients between twelve and sixteen years of age require the consent of their parents.)

Additional safeguards: The legislation provides for the establishment of regional review committees for termination of life on request and assisted suicide.

Each committee is composed of an uneven number of members: a legal expert, a doctor, and an expert in the field of ethics or philosophy.

The committees assess whether a case of termination of life on request or assisted suicide complies with the due diligence criteria. The committee is required to notify the physician of its findings and give their reasons.

Where a committee is of the opinion that the physician did not act in accordance with the criteria, the case must be brought to the attention of the Public Prosecution Service, which then has the power to launch a criminal investigation.

Regional committees have the capacity to personally discuss with the physician the assessment given and through annual reports contribute to public debate and awareness of termination of life on request and assisted suicide and the supervision exercised.

It should be noted that euthanasia remains a criminal offense in cases not meeting the law's specific conditions, with the exception of several situations (below) that are not subject to the restrictions of the law at all because they are considered normal medical practice of passive euthanasia, which is common throughout the Western world:

Stopping or not starting a medically useless (futile) treatment.

Stopping or not starting a treatment at the patient's request.

Speeding up death as a result of the necessary treatment to alleviate serious pain and suffering.

It is interesting to note that since March 2012, six specialised teams have been assigned to crisscross the Netherlands to carry out euthanasia at the homes of patients who are registered, who comply with legal criteria, and whose own doctors refuse to help them. If a patient complies with the legal criteria, a mobile team called the "Levenseinde" or "Life End" can be requested to carry out the euthanasia in the comfort of the patient's home. The teams are made up of specially trained doctors and nurses who work part time to visit patients all over the Netherlands. The mobile euthanasia plan has received the approval of the Dutch parliament and is expected to receive around 1,000 euthanasia requests per year.

In February 2010 a Netherlands citizens' initiative called Out of Free Will demanded that all Dutch people over seventy who feel tired of life should have the right to professional help in ending it. The organization started collecting signatures in support of this proposed change in legislation. A number of prominent Dutch citizens supported the initiative, including former ministers, artists, legal scholars, and physicians. Under current Dutch law, euthanasia by doctors is only legal in cases of hopeless and unbearable suffering. In practice this means it is limited to those suffering from serious medical conditions and in considerable pain. Helping somebody to commit suicide without meeting the qualifications of the current Dutch euthanasia law is illegal.

Access for minors: The legislation covers minors' requests for termination of life or assistance with suicide. A physician may comply with a request by a minor between the ages of twelve and sixteen if the patient is deemed capable of making a reasonable appraisal of his or her own interests and when the parents or guardians are unable to agree on the termination of life or assisted suicide.

With respect to minors between sixteen and eighteen, the legislation provides that a physician may comply with a request if the patient is deemed capable of making a reasonable appraisal of his or her own interests and the physician consults with the parents or guardians of the minor.

Access for people from other countries: The Netherlands Ministry of Justice believes it is not possible for people to come from other countries to seek termination of life or assistance with suicide in the Netherlands because of the legislation's procedural requirements. The procedure for the notification and assessment of each case requires the patient to have made a voluntary, considered request and to be suffering without any prospect of improvement. In order to be able to assess whether this is the case, the doctor must know the patient well and have treated the patient for some time. The practical aspect of this procedural requirement is subject to further review.

Generally, euthanasia tourism is associated with the pro-euthanasia movement, which organizes trips for potential suicide candidates to the few places where euthanasia is tolerated. In doing so, they hope to encourage the decriminalization of euthanasia and assisted suicide in many parts of the world.

The courage of the Dutch

It is a fact that the majority of people in the Netherlands support voluntary euthanasia. It is also a fact that willing doctors in the Netherlands have been participating in voluntary euthanasia for a considerable time. Furthermore, research suggests that a majority of people in civilized countries, including health professionals, support voluntary euthanasia and assisted suicide.

The enactment of the Netherlands' legislation represents the culmination of almost thirty years of public debate in that country. The nature and result of that discussion has been influenced by an arguably unique combination of social and cultural factors.

In the past euthanasia was prohibited according Article 293 of The Netherlands Penal Code, which provided that a person who took the life of another person at that person's "express and serious" request could be punished with imprisonment for a maximum of twelve years or with a fine. However, despite this fact, euthanasia has been regularly practiced since 1973. To justify what is admittedly an offense, courts in the Netherlands in many instances ruled that it was acceptable for a doctor, faced with the alternatives of leaving a patient in pain or giving relief by taking life, to take the compassionate option known as *force majeure* or necessity.

Under the new law, the public prosecutor has to prove the physician has not fulfilled the requirements if an order for prosecution is to commence. This is a significant shift. It may now be harder for prosecutors to proceed in doubtful cases, and effective control of euthanasia and the successful prosecution of unacceptable practices will become even more difficult and thus likely more uncommon.

The fear of some adverse outcome of the new law did not eventuate, and there is no doubt about the success of its implementation. It is prudent, however, for any country contemplating legalizing euthanasia and assisted suicide to ensure safety measures and scrutiny systems are in place. The Dutch legislation, which is not based on blind acceptance, should be a beacon to other secular countries. At the heart of the legislation is the well-being of the sick—not just some of them, but all. It gives the option to many religious and even some nonreligious people to carry anti-euthanasia cards, to ensure that their wishes are met when they are admitted to hospital in an emergency.

The "declaration of life" cards read: "I request that no medical treatment will be withheld on the grounds that the future quality of my life will be diminished... I request that under no circumstances is a life-ending treatment be administered because I am of the opinion that people do not have the right to end life."

These people, and others of like mind, will now be certain that their beliefs and wishes will always be respected. This is to counter the fear tactic that is usually unleashed by the religious industry against this aspect of the legislation. The legislation is in no way impinging the rights of religious believers, as can be seen from the Netherlands practice.

In conclusion, people around the world should have the courage of the Dutch to debate difficult moral issues by including the participation of doctors and their medical associations and their endorsement of the practice for termination of life on request or assisting with suicide.

Oregon's Death With Dignity Act

On November 8, 1994, the US state of Oregon approved the Death With Dignity Act (which went into effect in 1997), legalizing physician-assisted dying with certain restrictions. Passage of the act made Oregon the first US state and one of the first jurisdictions in the world to permit some terminally ill patients to determine the times of their own deaths.

Under the law a capable adult Oregon resident who has been diagnosed, by a physician, with a terminal illness that will kill him or her within six months may request in writing, from his or her physician, a prescription for a lethal dose of medication for the purpose of ending his or her own life. Exercise of the option under this law is voluntary, and the patient must initiate the request. Any physician, pharmacist, or health care provider who has moral objections may refuse to participate.

The request must be confirmed by two witnesses, at least one of whom is not related to the patient, is not entitled to any portion of the patient's estate, is not the patient's physician, and is not employed by a health care facility caring for the patient. After the request is made, another physician must examine the patient's medical records and confirm the diagnosis. The patient must be determined to be free of a judgment-impairing mental condition.

If the request is authorized, the patient must wait at least fifteen days and make a second oral request before the prescription maybe written. Should either physician have concerns about the patient's ability to make an informed decision or feel the patient's request may be motivated by depression or coercion; the patient must be referred for a psychological evaluation. The patient has a right to rescind the request at any time.

The law protects doctors from liability for providing lethal prescriptions for terminally ill, competent adults in compliance with the statute's restrictions. Participation by physicians, pharmacists, and health care providers is voluntary. The law also specifies a patient's decision to end his or her life shall not "have an effect upon a life, health, or accident insurance or annuity policy."

As part of the safeguards, the provisions for eligibility to use the Oregon's Death With Dignity Act include:

The person must be an adult (eighteen or over) resident of the state of Oregon.

The person must be mentally competent, verified by two physicians (or referred for a mental health evaluation).

The person must be terminally ill with less than six months to live, verified by two physicians.

The person must make voluntary requests, without coercion, verified by two physicians.

The person must be informed of all other options, including palliative and hospice care.

There is a fifteen-day waiting period between the first oral request and a written request.

There is a forty-eight-hour waiting period between the written request and the writing of the prescription.

The written request must be signed by two independent witnesses, at least one of whom is not related to the person or employed by the health care facility caring for the patient.

The person is encouraged to discuss the decision with family (though this is not required because of confidentiality laws).

The person may change his or her mind at any time and rescind the request.

The attending physician may sign the patient's death certificate, which must list the underlying terminal disease as the cause of death.

An independent study published in the October 2007 issue of the *Journal of Medical Ethics* made clear that there had been no negative impact since Oregon's act went into effect. There was no evidence of heightened risks for the elderly, women, the uninsured, and people with low educational statuses, the poor, the physically disabled or chronically ill, minors, and people with psychiatric illnesses including depression, or racial or ethnic minorities compared with background populations.

In addition, the fear that terminally ill people would flock to Oregon to take advantage of the law was not realized because the law limited its use to Oregon residents only.

It should be noted that Oregon's Death With Dignity Act doesn't permit physicians to administer lethal injections; it requires the patients to self-administer the final dosages. However, for emergency response, doctors and nurses are often requested to be present during the procedure. It is also worth noting that in Oregon the most successful legal prescription of lethal medicine used in assisted suicide is Nembutal in liquid form. (For methods, see chapter 8.)

Belgium's Euthanasia Legislation

Belgium's laws on euthanasia were adopted on May 16, 2002. In both Belgium and the Netherlands, the legality of euthanasia requires adherence to strict conditions and confirmation after a notification procedure. Although both laws are rather similar, the Belgian law is stricter on the requirements of prudent practice. In Belgium the law only applies to adults, whereas in the Netherlands minors over twelve years of age may, under certain conditions, receive euthanasia. However, the Belgian National Medical Disciplinary Board has recently mitigated the differences by drafting guidelines that reflect a broad interpretation of the law.

A major difference between the two countries is that in the Dutch society, the rules on euthanasia developed more through the science and philosophy of human law and endorsement by the medical association than through legislation.

The implementation of the law and the notification procedure in Belgium appears more difficult than in the Netherlands. In order to promote the quality of the euthanasia practice, the notification procedure in the Netherlands is followed by systematic feedback by and to the physicians. On the other hand, the strict anonymity of the Belgian notification procedure is broken only when the control commission finds some anomaly or deficiency in the declaration. Therefore, unless the commission makes ample use of its prerogative to contact physicians, the physicians may be less encouraged to improve their knowledge and skills in euthanasia.

In both countries physicians are required to notify a review committee of their cases, which should stimulate them to safeguard the quality of their euthanasia practices. It also makes control over the practice of euthanasia possible. However, the procedures in both countries differ. The main differences are that the Dutch notification and control procedures are more elaborate and transparent than the Belgian; the Belgian procedures are primarily anonymous. Evaluation is made in both countries through committees' summary reports to parliament.

In both countries transparent procedures, along with the information given to physicians about the law and the due care requirements for euthanasia and the systematic feedback about their medical actions, are pivotal to achieving efficient control and engendering the level of care needed when performing such far-reaching medical acts.

Switzerland's Euthanasia Laws

Euthanasia in Switzerland is illegal, but there is a heated debate about legalizing it. Assisted suicide and euthanasia raise questions that cannot be answered from the perspective of medicine alone. An incompatibility between euthanasia and assisted suicide on the one hand and the outdated physicians' Hippocratic Oath on the other may mean physicians should not assist death, but it does not necessarily settle the argument of whether anyone ever should. The controversy has remained intense. Acceptance of euthanasia and assisted suicide is growing as end-of-life issues are kept in the public eye. Further empirical analysis of this situation is important. This debate could continue to yield insights into the issues around suffering at the end of life.

In a 1999 survey of the Swiss public, eighty-two percent of respondents agreed that "a person suffering from an incurable disease and who has intolerable physical and psychological suffering has the right to ask for death and to obtain help for this purpose."

On the other hand, assisted suicide is legally condoned and can be preformed by non-physicians. The involvement of a physician is usually considered a necessary safeguard in assisted suicide, as is the case in countries and states where assisted suicide is legalized. Physicians are more qualified to know how to ensure a painless death, and they are in a position to offer palliative care as and when required. In 2001 the Swiss parliament rejected a bill that would have barred physicians from assisting suicide.

Switzerland seems to be the only country in which the law limits the circumstances in which assisted suicide is a crime, thereby decriminalizing it in other cases, without requiring the involvement of a physician. Consequently, non-physicians have participated in assisted suicide. The law has explicitly separated the issue of whether or not assisting death should be allowed in some circumstances from the issue of whether physicians should do it. This separation has not resulted in moral desensitization of assisted suicide and euthanasia.

Article 115 of the Swiss penal code considers assisting suicide a crime if and only if the motive is selfish. It condones assisting suicide for unselfish reasons. This reliance on a base motive rather than on the intent to kill to define a crime is foreign to the Anglo-Saxon legal system, but it can be pivotal in continental Europe. Swiss law does not consider suicide a crime or assisting suicide complicity in a crime. It views suicide as possibly rational. Also it does not give physicians special status in assisting it.

When an assisted suicide is declared, a police inquiry is started, as in all cases of unnatural death. Since no crime has been committed in the absence of a selfish motive, these are mostly open-and-shut cases. Prosecution happens if doubts are raised about the patient's competence to make an autonomous choice.

Swiss law, on the other hand, does not recognize the concept of euthanasia. Article 114 of the Swiss penal code treats murder upon request by the victim less severely than murder without the victim's request, but it remains illegal. (For more information on Switzerland and Dignitas, see chapter 8.)

Conclusion

Progressive governments contemplating the introduction of euthanasia laws in their countries can use the above euthanasia and assisted suicide laws as a guide and include further safeguards to satisfy their social tolerance and avoid religiously generated fear. For example a terminally ill patient requesting assisted suicide might be diagnosed and confirmed by more than two doctors and his or her pain and suffering assessment can be made by a psychiatrist and a counselor to ensure the patient is in sound mind and not in state of clinical depression. Additionally the patient's competence can be assessed on more than one occasion by all concerned, including a mandatory cooling-off period of two weeks. During the assessment period, the patient should be offered all alternatives, including palliative care and palliative sedation options.

Finally, ideally, the patient can be presented with the choice of the currently legalized end-of-life models: Oregon's, the Netherlands', and the palliative care. The palliative care model however, must include the option of physician assisted suicide besides the currently practiced palliative sedation.

All these additional measures are to ensure the system is not subjected to abuse and to silence the vocal anti-euthanasia, pro-life, and religious-rights groups.

Chapter 7

Case Studies

In the following stories, to avoid disclosing identities and to protect the privacy of individuals, their real names, their stories, dates, and locations have been changed. Some of the countries and states selected for the stories are real and some are not. Some of the stories are anonymous and some are reconstructed from publicized cases. However, the objective of the stories is to highlight the common thread between the mentioned countries and other similar ones that pretend to have secular systems of government when in fact they are under direct or indirect influence of the religious industry.

Their social and political policies are often hijacked by religious leaders, religious-right, pro-life, and right-to-life groups. These vocal minority groups are now the main stumbling block preventing the legalization of euthanasia and assisted suicide. They stifle the debate and in the process suppress human rights and freedom of choice by using their lobbying power and active campaigning. Religious leaders utilize their places of worship and religious schools to stir up emotions and place enormous pressure on politicians to toe their undemocratic and religious line. A country cannot claim to be secular when its agendas and policies are dictated by religion.

Ultra-conservative religious leaders should not be allowed to impose their religious dogmas on terminally ill patients who want nothing but the peaceful termination of their painful existences. The families of these patients also suffer, and many of them wish their loved ones would be allowed to pass away peacefully, with dignity and without pain.

Politicians in a secular and democratic country are meant to leave their religious dogmas at the door and out of citizens' lives. It is intended, in a multicultural, secular country that is not evangelical, Jewish, Buddhist, Hindu, Muslim, atheist, or Catholic, for politicians to be rational and not subservient to unelected religious leaders or hostage to an ideology. Politicians and religious leaders are entitled to follow any religion they wish, but they are not entitled to force their religions down everyone else's throats.

Governments and religious leaders should understand it is the democratic right of all citizens to decide what is best for themselves without the imposition of conservatism, religious dogmas, and outdated ideologies. Government and religious leaders should also understand they have neither the right nor the power to make people suffer. Governments have only the responsibility to produce secular laws to ensure patients' democratic and human rights are upheld.

Some liberated countries and states are in accord with the secular silent majority that is now more advanced in implementing better social programs and in adopting more-inclusive democratic systems of government. In some other semi-secular countries and states, however, the influence of religious leaders has become indirect. They are able to achieve their objectives by intense lobbying, threatening politicians with redirecting votes, or cultivating or implanting masquerading politicians in office to run the religious agenda on their behalf.

Fair-minded people should revolt against any politician who attempts to use religion as a tool to suppress freedom of choice and human rights. The silent majority should understand that the mutual benefits derived from the interdependency of religion and politics in this way is a backward step that leads to total dominance of religion over the country and citizens' lives. Religious leaders, being backward-looking, are capable and always have the desire to take their countries back into the distant past.

Accordingly, the silent majority should mobilize its forces and shed its apathy to counter the religious-rights onslaught on their future and the future of the next generation. (For more information, see chapter 6, "Religion and Culture," in my earlier book *Thorny Opinion*.)

Right-to-Die British Style

Sam, who had recently been diagnosed with advanced cancer, asked his son John for a favor: to help him commit suicide. At that time John, a car mechanic, knew his father was very sick and in unbearable pain, so he agreed to help.

On June 5, 2002 John helped his father to pass away peacefully. The cause of death was an overdose of morphine and carbon monoxide poisoning. No suspicious circumstances were detected. The death was self-inflicted because of cancer.

For more than nine years, John kept the secret to himself, until he decided to tell the world of what happened. His reconstructed and paraphrased story was told under the heading of "I had to help my dad commit suicide," in which he said:

> My father was seventy-six, a retired public servant, and my mother was seventy-two, a retired school teacher. They were both non-religious with scientific orientation. They believed in facts rather than fictions. They considered religion to be based on conjectures without tangible evidence. Above all, they believed in themselves rather than in an invented power in the sky. They were very active, happy, and filled with pride. When they became sick, their pride played a major role in their decision to end their lives with overdoses of medicines and my help. They knew they would be totally dependent on others in their last days of life. They also knew well that their government is indirectly controlled by religiously oriented politicians and other gutless, opportunistic politicians who, for self-preservation, choose to toe the religious line in fear of losing religious voters.
>
> In Britain patients in my parents' predicament have the right to refuse life-sustaining treatments

but they can't ask for assisted suicide or active, voluntary euthanasia. Alternatively they can travel to Switzerland as euthanasia tourists.

The High Court in various cases has held that in the case of assisted suicide, the interest of the state will prevail over an individual's interest. Therefore, all the country could offer them was palliative care, which to them meant they would be on the scrap heap of medical care. This is what usually happens when doctors run out of options—they condemn their patients to the mercy of establishments where painkillers are served, like heavy doses of morphine.

To my parents this was not what life was all about. They would rather have been dead than exist like that. They valued the quality of their lives enormously and this was not what they expected to end up like—bedridden, cared for by others, on constant pain killers, and, above all, a burden on me and my two sisters, who live with their families far away in other counties. I am the only son; I live close by. Both my wife and I work full-time to support our four young children.

Furthermore, they hated the thought of dying in hospital at a huge cost to the community and the health system. They often asked, what for? Is it just to be kept alive, bedridden and without dignity for more days or more weeks? Would their final existences be to occupy hospital beds and compete with other patients who had better chances of recovery? Was this what was life about?

They simply would not accept it, and they knew what they wanted. Since euthanasia and assisted suicide are still illegal in Britain, there was nothing left for them other than committing suicide. No matter how cruel and inhumane it is, the religious industry and the gutless politicians are happy to live with the concept of suicide, rather than do the right thing for desperate patients, as is the case in some more progressive countries and states like Belgium, the Netherlands, the American state of Oregon, and so on.

All my parents wanted was to die without pain and with dignity. With no reasonable option left, they turned to me for help. My love for them and my belief in humanity made me decide to respond to their cries for help. Seeing them so helpless when they made their wishes so clear to me, I felt I had no option. Our family, as well as the majority in Britain, believe in human rights and freedom of choice, unlike the vocal religious leaders and pro-life fanatics who bring pressure to bear on politicians in a country where religion and state are meant to be separate. Their influence on the majority is a cruel punishment for the terminally ill people who choose to die serenely and with dignity.

What is the purpose of making my parents endure the pain and agony for a few more days or few more weeks? I wondered. Was it just to satisfy the dogmatic and hypocritical ultraconservative theologians who dictate the outdated "death is in the hands of God" dogma to the enlightened people of the world? How can these dogmatic leaders convince proud people like my parents, who would soon be in a vegetative state, on life-support machines, and soiling themselves to believe there is, somewhere in the sky, a dictator that must be obeyed?

When my dad called me in for a chat, I had an inkling he wanted to talk about his predicament. Nevertheless I was startled when he directly said, "Please help me." Lying in bed, looking straight in my eyes, in a measured and smooth voice he said, "Son, I'm dying. I don't have more than few weeks at most. But I do have an option about how and when my death will occur. I'm already taking morphine as a painkiller. If I double or triple the dose that should do the trick without anyone knowing or getting upset."

I realized what he meant. But as powerful as his words were, the idea behind them didn't seem strange at all. It made sense. He was about to die anyway, so why linger in pain? I knew I'd want to do the same thing if I were in his position. I didn't know what to say, so I kept quiet and waited for him to continue. I don't know if I could have said anything even if I'd wanted to, because I was still somewhat stunned not only by the intensity of what he had told me but because I had never expected him to share thoughts like these with me.

He continued, "My cancer is well advanced. If I die early, nobody is going to notice, and I'll have saved myself a hell of a lot of pain. This is why I need your help."

With a sinking heart, I said, "Dad, I will do anything you ask. Are you in a lot of pain? What happens next?"

"Well," he said, and then sighed heavily. "I feel pain all over. My next step would be to start the new regimes of chemotherapy and radiation, but I'm not sure I want to subject myself to that."

Dozens of thoughts jumped through my head, but I tried to focus and concentrate on practical matters. "What about Mom? How is she holding up?"

"She's okay for now, but she's putting on a brave face. I know she's worried as hell, and, of course, I'm worried about her too. Her health isn't the best. That's something else you and I will have to discuss later." Mom was afflicted with Lou Gehrig's disease.

To help Dad with suicide, I had to think deeply about the complexities of my role and keep calm. My participation would lead to legal issues and facing a jury trial without knowing what the outcome would be. No matter what, my job of helping Dad was more important than any other consideration. My promise to him had to be fulfilled. He wasn't only my father but my best friend—had been my whole life.

On his seventy-sixth birthday, all the family gathered around him to cheer him up and wish him the best, but unfortunately everybody knew it would be his last birthday. My mom gathered all her strength to hide her debilitating conditions and be cheerful for him. The party went as well as expected, with smiles all around. I felt my heart was burning, but I had to show a brave face.

After my sisters, their husbands, and their children left, my mom and I sat beside Dad's bed and held his hands, and the three of us burst into spontaneous and uncontrollable tears. It was as if we were saying our final goodbyes when Dad was in no mood to leave us yet. Suddenly I remembered my role was to keep everybody calm and comfortable, so first I helped Mom to her bed and then came back to Dad's side. I knew he wanted to have a serious talk about his plan for dealing with his rapidly advancing cancer.

He said, "Son, I know my number is up. There's no cure for my cancer, and if there is a cure it will be worse than the disease. I don't want to have any further treatment, and I don't want to have any form of palliative care. That's for people who don't know the difference between living and existing, or for others who are scared of death, or for some who are blindly religious. I'm none of those. Despite the fact that occasionally I can go out or drive the car for short distances, I can't stand the thought of being condemned to bed doing nothing but suffering. What's the point? Just to exist for more days or weeks and make your mom suffer with me? I hate that thought, especially knowing her Lou Gehrig's disease is getting worse."

Despite our earlier emotional episode, Dad and I possessed a high degree of will power and the ability to face reality. Though our conversation gathered more intensity, we remained calm and tried to support each other in our usual behavioral patterns. Although, I must admit, deep inside I felt like I was putting on an appearance to keep his spirit high, because I knew he was about to bring the conversation to a critical point. I also knew it would be very hard for him to talk about the painful subject, so I decided to wade in.

I said, "Listen, Dad, I know why you're telling me all this and I know we have important and unfinished business to talk about regarding your deteriorating condition. I've been thinking about the situation since you told me your cancer has spread. Can you now tell me about your plan?"

I sensed he was bracing himself, and then he relaxed. He said, "Thank you, son. You don't know how relieved I am. My plan is to overdose on morphine, but to avoid any pain or complication; I will need your help with asphyxiation. If you can, set up the gas exhaust to run into the car. The morphine and the carbon monoxide will do the job. It will look like a suicide and nobody will know."

The next day the father's body was found in his car. He was on his way back from a visit to his son's house. The cause of death was suicide because of advanced cancer. Six months later his wife's body was found in her bed. The cause of death was suicide because of advanced Lou Gehrig's disease.

Right-to-Die Italian Style

On February 6, 2009, a right-to-die case triggered an Italian crisis. Italy's government issued an emergency decree to prevent the death of Eluana Englaro, who was in a vegetative state from having her feeding tubes disconnected. President Giorgio Napolitano immediately said he wouldn't sign it. As a result Englaro's family vowed to go ahead and disconnect the tubes. Her nutritional intake was being reduced in preparation.

President Napolitano said the government decree was unconstitutional since it violated the fundamental separation of power between the executive and judicial branches. He said it defied court rulings that favored removing Englaro's feeding tubes.

Premier Silvio Berlusconi insisted the decree was urgent since procedures to disconnect Englaro's feeding tubes had begun. Given the president's refusal to sign the decree, Berlusconi said he would, in the next two to three days, ask parliament, where he had a solid majority, to turn the decree into law.

The bitter right-to-die debate divided Italy and prompted direct appeals by the Vatican to keep Englaro alive. She had been in a vegetative state—a coma—for seventeen years, since a car accident in 1992. She was twenty at the time of the accident. Two years later doctors called her condition irreversible. Her father won a protracted court battle to disconnect her feeding tube, which he said had been her wish.

The government's decree, passed at a cabinet meeting, states that feeding and hydrating patients who depend on it "can in no case be suspended." Berlusconi said, "I would feel responsible for failing to come to the rescue of somebody whose life was in danger." He added, "The government had decided to intervene because Englaro was moved to a clinic in northern Italy that agreed to gradually stop feeding her." The transfer set off a firestorm, with appeals from anti-euthanasia groups and Catholic Church officials to keep her alive.

Italy does not allow euthanasia. Patients have a right to refuse treatment, but there is no law that allows them to give advance directions on what treatments they wish to receive if they become unconscious.

The Englaro case drew comparisons to that of Terri Schiavo, the American woman who was at the center of a right-to-die debate until her death in 2005 in the state of Florida. Schiavo's feeding tube was removed in March 2005 after she had been in coma for fifteen years. Congress passed a bill to allow a federal court to review her case. A federal judge refused to order the tube reinserted, a decision upheld by a federal appeals court and the Supreme Court.

In Italy, before the government's decree could be approved, the president said the fundamental separation of power between the executive and judicial branches needed to be safeguarded. He cited the decision a year earlier by Italy's highest court that effectively put its seal of approval on a lower court's ruling allowing the feeding tube to be removed.

In explaining the need for the decree, Berlusconi urged doctors and relatives to rethink their decision, which he described as "the killing of a human being who is still alive." He described Englaro as somebody who could even "bear a child and who is in a vegetative state that could change."

Eluana's family were undeterred, even though the government sent inspectors to the facility in the north-eastern city of Udine where she was being cared for. Vittorio Angiolini, the family's lawyer, said he was certain the family was acting within the law, described the decree as an "abnormal measure," and praised the president's stance as "impeccable."

The Vatican, on the other hand, praised the government. Elio Sgreccia, a top official with the Vatican's Pontifical Academy for Life, told the ANSA news agency that Englaro "has the right to live." He added, "The political community must sustain her life with the means it has."

Pope Benedict XVI intervened indirectly in the case, saying euthanasia was "a false solution to suffering that [is]n't worthy of humans."

It might be noted that president Napolitano's political career has been marked by moderation and moral rigor, and as president he was expected to be above the political fray to safeguard the constitution. As a result, the conflict between him and the government appeared to have more to do with Berlusconi asserting the power of the executive branch (especially in appeasing the Vatican) and the president holding him in check rather than any personal squabble based on traditional political lines.

Eluana Englaro, the comatose accident victim at the center of a right-to-die drama that gripped Italy, died while the government was debating a bill to force doctors to restore her life support. This occurred when the doctors in Udine stopped feeding the thirty-eight-year-old woman amid a flurry of efforts to keep her from dying, with opportunistic, conservative Prime Minister Silvio Berlusconi accused of politicizing the affair. The Vatican reacted swiftly to the news of Englaro's death, saying, "May the Lord welcome her and forgive those who led her there [to her death]."

This is the contrast in Italy, where euthanasia is illegal, but patients have the right to refuse medical care. In Englaro's case it is even worse. Italian courts said they were satisfied that her coma was irreversible. Furthermore, she had clearly expressed her wish not to be kept alive artificially after a close friend of hers fell into coma following an accident. Her treating doctors felt they were doing the right thing in assisting her death. They were helping her achieve her own wish as a defenseless person who was betrayed by the government and the church. Yet she has become a symbol for the Catholic Church in its campaign against passive euthanasia.

The irony is: Her case has torn the predominantly religious Catholic country in two. Fifty-three percent of adult Italians surveyed were in favor of her dying and forty-seven percent wanted her kept alive. This is worrisome in Italy, where politics and religion are inseparable and where human stories can be exploited by the church and the government.

Right-to-Die Australian Style

In September 2009 a forty-nine-year-old Australian quadriplegic man named Kevin Stanley won the right to starve himself to death. A series of injuries had made Stanley a spastic quadriplegic a year earlier, and he described his life as a "living hell." He had asked his carers at least forty times to stop feeding and hydrating him through a tube to his stomach before the matter was taken to court.

His lawyer, John Hammond, took his case to the Supreme Court to see if his wishes to stop being fed artificially could be fulfilled legally. The Supreme Court ruled Stanley could ask his carers to stop treating him if he understood the consequences of his request. The landmark ruling effectively gave him an avenue to die by starving to death.

However, the ruling was not about euthanasia but about giving people the right to refuse treatment if they are dying. His case set an important precedent that prompted more people to seek similar rulings. More often people in a lot of physical discomfort have started to ask their doctors and nursing staff to help them leave this world with dignity.

Stanley is now remembered as someone who was very brave and took up a fight that will give a lot of people comfort. He set the means by which people could exit life with dignity, something he was very keen to do. It is easy to understand how terrible it is for people in his position to feel each day that life no longer has any value and is full of pain and suffering. His case and other mercy killing cases don't belong in the normal aspect of life.

Another mercy killing case wherein a man was prosecuted for helping his wife commit suicide when she was suffering from a debilitating disease should not have been a case under criminal law. The man took the action with love and dedication to his partner with her full consent to surrender her right to life.

Stanley's case, on the other hand, demonstrated that people with legitimate human rights issues have to resort to courts to achieve their desired outcomes while others who don't have the means to hire lawyers to fight for their rights are left behind to suffer and are discriminated against.

Australia is one of the so-called civilized countries where democracy is influenced by Christian lobby groups who can dictate to gutless politicians their religious agendas. Unfortunately, it will get worse with the demise of its moderate government and the emergence of the extreme-right conservatives. The reactionary, extreme-right groups are now in control of the conservative Liberal Party, which is the mirror image of the extremist groups that are the driving force behind the Tea Party in America. (For more on the Tea Party, see chapter 2 of my earlier book *Israel vs. America vs. the World*.)

In 1997 the same reactionary elements in the Australian government decided to overturn the euthanasia laws of the Australian Northern Territories. In the name of religion, these dark forces are causing unnecessary agony to their fellow humans and distress to honest and dedicated people who are driven by humanity to assist patients to pass away without pain and with dignity.

The following two Australian cases of mercy killing are good illustrations of why religion shouldn't be the stumbling block preventing the legalization of euthanasia and assisted suicide.

David Clark's case: The police asked David Clark, who killed his sixty-eight-year-old wife, Eva, to elaborate on his earlier statement to them, in which he said, "Eva was in constant pain, suffering from a degenerative spinal condition, and wanted to commit suicide." He replied: "She had tried to overdose on antidepressants, and I had to help end her life when, two days later, she was still alive... If I wasn't facing you having committed the crime, I'd be facing her... Why didn't I do something when I could?"

Later, in court, he said, "I was torn between love and respect for her and the temptation to end her pain. My action was born out of exceptional circumstances and a cry for compassion... Suffering constant pain from osteoarthritis, Eva twice overdosed on antidepressant pills in the twenty-four hours before she died at her home in July 2009."

According to a clinical pharmacological report, the amount of drugs she had taken probably put her on the road to death. But it seems the end did not come soon enough. Clark put a plastic bag over her head and suffocated her. After his arrest he told detectives he had wanted to spare her from continuing pain. "I finished what she started," he said. "I think she had pretty much made up her mind then because she thought if things got to the stage where she had to go into a nursing home, then this ability to take control of her destiny would be taken from her."

Clark, sixty-six, pled guilty to manslaughter on the grounds of substantial mental impairment following psychiatric examinations by the prosecutor and the defense. The prosecutor, Mervin Stone, told the Supreme Court that he would not seek a full-time jail term for Clark. Anything Clark did was an act of love. Drawn together by their shared love of music, bushwalking, and the environment, Clark and his wife had been together for thirty-two years. Friends described them as a loving couple, committed to good causes and to each other.

Eva was very anxious not to be dependent on people. If there had been some proper process in place, like legalized assisted suicide, she wouldn't have had to go through a bad death. Her loss of autonomy, loss of the ability to engage in activities that make life enjoyable, and the suffering she had gone through prompted her to take drastic action.

In his sentencing submissions in the Supreme Court, Judge Allen Smith said, "This was not a case for punishment, or one in which the community needed protection. The offender's crime was born out of selfless love, not evil, and motivated by relief of suffering of the deceased."

Prosecutor Mervin Stone, in seeking a suspended sentence, acknowledged that had Clark not "openly and honestly admitted to police what had occurred, we wouldn't be here."

David Scott Clark was handed a suspended sentence of two years for the manslaughter of Eva Clark in 2009. He was also put on a two-year good-behavior bond. The man who had suffocated his chronically ill partner with a plastic bag avoided jail, with the judge saying, "He was the person she loved more than anyone else. That presented the offender with an agonizing conflict."

Supreme Court Justice Peter Buchan said the pair's relationship was one of shared happiness and devotion, and Mrs. Clark had spoken to her husband about ending her life due to constant pain from a spine condition. Justice Buchan also said, "Mr. Clark was suffering substantial impairment at the time he committed the crime, but it was a selfless act, born out of love [he] had for her. This was not a case of one person making a decision for another."

Ron and Mary Beresford's case: After more than sixty years together, Australian couple Ron and Mary Beresford decided to end their lives together. They were an exemplary loving, married couple who never wanted to be apart. In a video recording they outlined their decision to end their lives together.

Euthanasia campaign group Exit International said the couple took doses of Nembutal on Sunday evening and were found dead in their home, holding hands.

Ron, eighty-two, had mesothelioma (a lung cancer caused by his earlier exposure to asbestos) while Mary, eighty-five, was not terminally ill but said she suffered from a lot of ailments of old age.

As members of Exit International, they made the video to make their story public. In the video Ron said the thought of being able to die with his wife after a wonderful life together gave him a great sense of peace, especially after living with a difficult disease. "I am confined to bed and after three years reached the point where my quality of life is dreadful," he said. "I'm dependent on Mary and my world has shrunk to this small bedroom. This is no life to live."

Mary said the couple's family had been supportive and they had come to the decision on their own, with no encouragement from anyone. "I want to be with Ron now and always. We plan to drink the drugs together and die together," she said. "Some people may criticize us for taking this step, but I can say we made the decision together after a lot of consideration, and we're clear it is the right decision for both of us."

After Ron's diagnosis in 2008, the couple travelled to Mexico to obtain the drug. "We both very much resented the fact that we had to travel halfway around the world just to have the choice. We should have been able to get this drug at our local pharmacy to be put safely away just in case of the necessity in the future."

It is worth noting that on September 26, 2011, Dr. Nitschke got permission to import the drug Nembutal to Australia for a voluntary euthanasia of a woman in South Australia. Hopefully, this permission will set a trend for the future. Some desperate Australians who are terminally ill and physically or financially impaired and unable to travel to Mexico will stay discriminated against until doctors are allowed to prescribe Nembutal for a peaceful end of life.

In Mexico, Nembutal, a barbiturate used to commit suicide, can be bought legally or on the black market. Although opinion polls indicate more than eighty percent of Australians would like the right to end their own lives if afflicted by terminal illnesses, it is illegal to import barbiturates, which are widely considered the best method. The drugs are used in many countries and states where euthanasia and assisted suicide are legal. In Switzerland, Luxembourg, Belgium, the Netherlands, and the US states of Washington, Oregon, and Montana, it is common for doctors to prescribe drugs to terminate the lives of terminally ill patients who have less than six months left to live.

On the other hand, in many countries, it is shocking to observe how, in desperate cases, the medical profession is determined to keep patients alive no matter what only because assisted suicide is illegal, which is aggravated by the availability of the latest invasive treatments that keep patients alive at all costs. Some doctors may not follow a patient's wishes to stop life-prolonging treatment because of their training, the outdated Hippocratic Oath, or their religious beliefs. The majority, however, accept that helping suffering patients at the ends of their lives is an acceptable and humane way of dealing with approaching death.

Furthermore, in countries where assisted suicide is illegal, sometimes courageous and humanitarian doctors covertly assist patients who are suffering terribly to die. Some other doctors champion the autonomy of dying patients and raise awareness of the right to opt out of invasive, time-consuming, or painful treatment. Unfortunately however, as stated above, there is variation in the degree to which people's wishes are respected. It is about, when the end comes, supporting the dying process through clearer guidance on withdrawing or withholding treatment. People with long-term diseases such as cancer, heart disease, or dementia sometimes end up in hospital, and there is never any discussion about what it all means. Raising the prospect of death earlier could conflict with the aims of intensive treatment.

Politicians who allow this state of confusion and allow doctors to apply the law unevenly are driven by unelected, vocal, religious lobby, pro-life, and right-to-life groups. The slogans of these religious dictators mean "life must be prolonged at all costs, regardless of quality" and "changing the laws will lead to a slippery slope." Their often-repeated argument is that changing legislation will lead to a significant increase in suicide.

Evidence from the Netherlands, where voluntary euthanasia has in effect been legal for several decades, suggests this won't happen. In the Netherlands' Department of Public Health, published reports indicate deaths from voluntary euthanasia, as a proportion of all deaths in the Netherlands, were approximately 1.8 percent. No reported cases indicated there was evidence of a slippery slope either generally or among especially vulnerable groups such as the poor and the mentally ill.

The Oregon experience also reflects this. There was no evidence the legalization of assisted suicide had led to an increase in suicides or put pressure on patients, especially the poor, to end their lives prematurely to save money. For better or worse, the laws are being used mostly by educated middle and upper class citizens.

Right-to-Die German Style

In Berlin in 2010, seventy-five-year-old Roger Schmitt, a euthanasia campaigner, assisted his eighty-five-year-old wife Carla to die. The unusual part of the case is that Carla was neither sick nor dying. She simply didn't want to move into a nursing home, and rather than face that prospect she asked her husband to assist her with a serene death.

Her last words, as recounted later by her husband, after swallowing a deadly cocktail of the anti-malaria drug chloroquine and the sedative diazepam, were, "Good night, darling." The ensuing publicity generated by her husband set off a national controversy over the limits on the right to die in a country that has struggled with the issue of mercy killing, especially because of what happened during the Nazis' rule, when at least 100,000 mentally disabled and terminally ill people were euthanized.

In an interview the justice minister of Bavaria said, "This woman had nothing wrong other than her fear. Her husband didn't offer her any other options." Germany's conservative Chancellor Angela Merkel declared on a German news channel on the same day, "I am absolutely against any form of assisted suicide, in whatever guise it comes."

Furthermore, Bavaria and four other German states are pushing for new laws to ban commercial ventures that help people kill themselves. Suicide itself is not a crime, nor is aiding a suicide provided it does not cross the line into euthanasia or mercy killing.

Some people do not want Germany to follow the example of Switzerland, where liberal laws on euthanasia have led to a bustling trade in assisted suicide. In the last decade, nearly 500 Germans have crossed the border to end their lives with the help of Swiss group Dignitas, which facilitates suicides. The religious lobby groups want to make it illegal for people to offer "suicide by reservation."

By helping Carla end her life and then broadcasting the result, Roger in effect declared that he would help other people like her who decided of their own free will to commit suicide. In a telephone interview, Roger said, "My offer is to allow people to die in their own bed. That is the wish of most people, and now it is possible in Germany."

With his penchant for brazen publicity, Roger recalls Jack Kevorkian, the euthanasia crusader in Michigan who all but dared the authorities to stop his assisted suicides and ended up in prison. But Roger, who is trained as a lawyer, is careful not to cross the legal line. In his wife's case, he counselled her about how to commit suicide but did not provide or administer the drugs. He videotaped five hours of interviews with his wife in which she discussed her fears and why she wanted to die.

He left the room after she drank the poisonous brew and returned three hours later to find her dead in her bed. He videotaped the entire process as proof that he was not an active participant. Prosecutors have looked into his case and found that he is not in breach of the law.

While Carla was not suffering from a life-threatening disease or in acute pain, her life was hardly pleasant, Roger said. She had trouble moving around the house and lived in fear of strangers. A nursing home seemed the likely next stop. When she decided to commit suicide, she contacted Dignitas, the Swiss group that aids suicides. She did that knowing Germany's laws didn't allow for enough dignity; they forced those assisting with suicides to leave the people to die alone or risk being prosecuted. In Switzerland, on the other hand, the helping person, as well as family members or friends, can stay with the person who has decided to die with dignity.

Carla's solitary death should teach Germany how to treat its old people. The fear of nursing homes among elderly Germans is far greater than the fear of terrorism or the fear of death. As a matter of fact, this is common of the elderly throughout the Western world. Nursing homes should be converted into palliative care hospices for the terminally ill and for people who fear death, especially religious people who wish to live till the last breath and the ones who believe only God who gives life can take it away.

The other lesson for Germany and the rest of the Western world is to follow the Netherlands' experience in allowing people to die with dignity and to legalize euthanasia and assisted suicide. For many people the alternative is for hospices to first, be affordable to all, and second, to introduce the practice of assisted suicide as a supplementary method to palliative sedation.

Right-to-Die American Style

Notes:

First, the following is not related to the states of Oregon, Washington, and Montana, where assisted suicide is legalized.

Second, on April 3, 1996, the US 2nd Circuit Court of Appeals declared unconstitutional a State of New York law that criminalized physician-assisted suicide for terminally ill patients. A panel of three judges found the law violated the equal protection guaranteed by the Fourteenth Amendment to the US Constitution. This ruling only affected three states: Connecticut, New York, and Vermont. On April 18, 1996, the attorney general of the state of New York asked that the ruling be suspended for a short time while the State appealed the decision to the US Supreme Court. The decision of the court was overturned by the US Supreme Court on June 26, 1997. They found the average American has no constitutional right to a physician-assisted suicide. Thus the New York laws that banned such suicides were constitutional. On the other hand, the court implied there is no constitutional bar that would prevent a state from passing a law permitting physician-assisted suicide. Oregon, Washington, and Montana have done exactly this.

The following case relates to the state of New York.

Fifty-five-year-old Jeff Brown was suffering from AIDS-related dementia. He was bedbound, unconscious, and permanently attached to a ventilator. He was totally incapacitated, which made him unable to make any decision or direct the doctors caring for him in one of New York's hospitals. He had no friends or family members and no identified relatives. His personal history had vanished into the maze of health care facilities he had been to in the last two years. Other than his name, Social Security number, and date of birth, his life story had disappeared.

Brown was one of thousands of physically devastated, mentally incompetent New Yorkers without hope of recovery. He had no next of kin, and there was nobody who could legally sanction a course of treatment. Even if friends or relatives were found, New York prohibits the withholding or withdrawing of life-sustaining treatment without a signed health care proxy or "clear and convincing" evidence of a patient's wishes. A "do not resuscitate" order can be put in place by doctors but only in the absence of identified next of kin and only if resuscitation is considered futile.

Some states, to varying extents, allow family members, friends, or guardians to make decisions about life support even without the knowledge of a patient's prior wishes. In the absence of a next of kin, only a few states grant doctors the ability to withdraw long-term life support systems from patients in vegetative states (when treatment preserves a heartbeat but offers no hope of recovery). New York, unfortunately, is not one of the states that offers this possibility, and doctors don't want to find themselves setting precedents for test cases on patients' rights to be treated or not treated.

In New York, just to mention the idea of withholding or withdrawing medical care from patients who cannot express their wishes makes all hell breaks loose. Advocacy groups, like right-to-life and pro-life movements and other religious fanatics, immediately use the term *medical killing* on the grounds that doctors have no right to judge the value of life. Only God who gives life can take it away. Regardless of any prognosis, life must be preserved till the last breath.

Unfortunately, these are the people who control the legal, social, and political agendas. This is despite the fact that, based on intensive studies, the majority of people and doctors are in favor of withholding or withdrawing life support from critically or terminally ill patients even without their knowledge.

It is interesting to note that many hospitals place great monetary value on patients like Brown. He was a valuable commodity. A ventilator-dependent patient, especially one undergoing the surgical incision necessary for long-term vent support, is among the highest-paying under Medicare's prospective hospital reimbursement system; his need for skilled care outside the hospital also made him a lucrative nursing home patient. Prognosis is not a factor in this equation. Forever on life support without hope of recovery, Brown would develop pneumonias, urinary infections, and other complications, each requiring transfer from the nursing home to the hospital, stabilization, and transfer back again. The providers would be reimbursed for each of these procedures.

Despite the advances made in the treatment of AIDS, Brown's dementia worsened, as did his terrible wasting and bedsores. Despite a full volley of high-tech interventions, he died without ever having done anything wilfully—not even eating, talking, or making eye contact. His well-intentioned hospital and doctors, fully aware of his dismal prognosis, had continued the excruciating process of inserting pencil-thick IV catheters and cleaning his fist-size bed sores.

It is doubtful Brown wanted these extreme interventions, and the American medical and ethical systems owed him a better way.

Chapter 8

Pro-Euthanasia
Organizations and
Methods

Notes: <u>First</u>, for ethical and moral reasons, and to skirt prohibition laws, humane doctors accept the fact that assisting a suffering and terminally ill patient to die peacefully is critical for their consciences. To avoid the legal implications, they discreetly recommend an overdose of morphine and sedative for unconsciousness, coupled with dehydration. Peaceful death could take a week or two when using this method.

    <u>Second</u>, in the majority of Western countries, doctors are operating under prohibition laws that exclude them from participating in ending the lives of patients except for

disconnecting life-support systems when there is no hope of survival. In other hopeless cases, when terminally ill patients are in unbearable pain and nearing the ends of their lives, doctors live with the dilemmas of helping their patients or abandoning them at a critical time. Some doctors, for legal or religious reasons, abandon the patients, while compassionate doctors take the risk and help patients in desperate need. Therefore, and very often, the prohibition laws and the current outdated Hippocratic Oath act against the patients' and the community's interests. Generally, prohibition laws discourage communication between the doctor and the dying patient and sometimes result in covert action on compassionate grounds.

Third, the information in this chapter is not intended to break any law of any country and should be used as a preliminary guide only. It is a summary of information found in many books and on websites and is provided in good faith. Before coming to a final conclusion, readers are advised to further examine all aspects of the course of action that might suit their situation and what advice is given by their physicians. In the first instance, a doctor who places God ahead of the patient should be avoided because the patient is unlikely to get objective advice and might end up suffering more. Furthermore, at the critical stage, the patient is likely to be abandoned on legal and religious grounds. The best choice for suffering and terminally ill patients nearing the ends of their lives is doctors who are driven by compassion. These doctors are amongst the majority who prefer and campaign for the legalization of euthanasia and assisted suicide.

Fourth, the pro-euthanasia organizations and the underground methods of ending life described below would not need to exist if the so-called civilized countries and their gutless politicians produced suitable laws with strict guide-lines legalizing euthanasia and assisted suicide. It is now well-established that a model based on the Netherlands' laws for euthanasia and another based on Oregon's laws for assisted suicide, which is complemented by an excellent palliative care system, is the best way forward, especially if pallia-tive care is expanded to include physician-assisted suicide. Politicians in backward countries and states are producing prohibition laws that create pain and desperation for termi-nally ill people. Bad politicians don't understand they have no right to make people suffer; instead they have a duty to produce suitable laws with safeguards to ensure citizens' hu-man rights and freedom of choice are upheld.

Fifth, all suffering and terminally ill patients who are nearing the end of life, together with their families and friends, must become active campaigners for the legalization of euthanasia and assisted suicide. Countering the religious slippery slope slogan and becoming as vocal as the ultracon-servative theologians who promote prohibitions is the only way to get politicians to take notice and act. Politicians only understand something when they sense their political surviv-al is at stake. Every person, young and old, must understand that the subject of legalization of euthanasia and assisted suicide has or will have direct impact on them. Everyone, at some stage, could be in a desperate predicament when their pain is so great that life will become meaningless. Politicians don't usually respond to the apathy of the majority. Instead they respond to the vocal and well-organized minority. It is now time for you to act. The futures of the following genera-tions, your human rights, and freedom of choice are at stake.

Warning: Except for under the direction of Dignitas and Exit International, in the absence of a doctor's supervision, most of the described methods could make the terminally ill patient suffer more and in some cases could result in violent death. To avoid the pitfalls, consultation with any of the pro-euthanasia organizations listed below is essential before contemplating any course of action. It is unfortunate that sometimes misleading suicide information is available on the Internet and elsewhere; it defeats the purpose of prohibiting doctors from assisting suffering patients whose only solution is death by suicide with an unpredictable outcome. The prohibition creates a dangerous environment for despairing people in their attempts to end their lives.

Dignitas Switzerland

PO Box 9
8127 Forch, Switzerland
Phone: + 4143 366 1070
E-mail: dignitas@dignitas.ch

Dignitas is a Swiss assisted-dying group that helps those with severe and terminal illnesses to die assisted by qualified doctors and nurses. Additionally, they provide suicide assistance for people provided they are of sound judgment and submit to an in-depth examination by a psychiatrist that establishes the patient's condition, as required by Swiss courts.

Dignitas's motto is: "To live with dignity—to die with dignity." It is constituted in accordance with Swiss law and was founded on May 17, 1998 at Forch (near Zurich). Its founder is Ludwig A. Minelli, a Swiss lawyer. Swiss laws provide that assisting a suicide is only illegal if it is motivated by self-interest. As a result Dignitas seeks to ensure it acts as a neutral party by proving that aside from non-recurring fees, they have nothing to gain from the deaths of its members.

Dignitas pursues no commercial interests whatsoever, in accordance with its constitution and to ensure the dignity of life and death for its members. It helps people from all over the world who seek its counseling. It is a member of the World Federation of Right-to-Die Societies. Some of its activities include:

Counseling members and non-members in regard to all end-of-life issues

Cooperating with physicians, clinics, and other associations

Carrying out patients' instructions and patients' rights with regard to doctors and clinics

Prevention of suicide and suicide attempts.

Supporting patients in conflicts with the authorities, management of nursing homes, and doctors not chosen by the patients.

Additionally, Dignitas helps its members with the preparation of their legally effective advance directives, which are respected by doctors and hospital nursing staff. In case of an illness that will lead inevitably to death, unendurable pain, or an unendurable disability, Dignitas offers its members the possibility of an accompanied suicide.

A person who wishes to die meets several Dignitas personnel, in addition to an independent doctor, for a private consultation. The doctor assesses the evidence provided by the patient on two separate occasions, with a time gap between each of the consultations. Legally admissible proof that the person wishes to die is also created by signing an affidavit that is countersigned by independent witnesses. In cases where people are physically unable to sign the documents, short videos are made in which they are asked to confirm their identity, that they wish to die, and that their decisions are made of their own free will, without any form of coercion. This evidence of informed consent remains private and is preserved only for use in any possible legal dispute.

Finally, a few minutes before the lethal overdose is provided, the person is once again reminded that taking the overdose will surely kill him or her. Additionally, he or she is asked several times whether he or she wants to proceed or take some time to consider the matter further. This gives the person the opportunity to stop the process. However, if at this point the person states he or she is determined to proceed, a lethal overdose is provided and ingested.

In general, Dignitas uses the following protocol to assist suicides: an oral dose of an antiemetic drug (effective against vomiting and nausea and typically used to treat motion sickness and as a general anesthetic), followed approximately thirty minutes later by a lethal overdose of powdered pentobarbital (typical prescription of fifteen grams of Nembutal powder) dissolved in a glass of water or fruit juice. If necessary the drugs can be ingested via a drinking straw. The pentobarbital overdose depresses the central nervous system, causing the person to become drowsy and fall asleep within ten minutes. When the anesthesia induces a coma, the person's breathing becomes shallower. Death is caused by respiratory arrest, which occurs within thirty minutes of ingesting the pentobarbital.

In a few cases in 2008, Dignitas used breathing helium gas as a suicide method instead of a pentobarbital overdose. Some people believe hypoxic death caused by helium is less peaceful than pentobarbital ingestion and causes shaking and twitching.

Costs and finances: Swiss law forbids any organization to profit from the act of aiding a suicide. Therefore, Dignitas is a not-for-profit organization. According to Ludwig Minelli, Dignitas charges its patients 4,000 Euros (approximately) for preparation and suicide assistance, or 7,000 Euros (approximately) in the case of taking over family duties including funerals, medical costs, and official fees.

Suicide tourism: Although the assisted suicide market is largely German, it is becoming very popular with British citizens who are clamoring to die at one of Dignitas's rented apartments in Zurich. In the absence of assisted suicide laws in many European and other Western countries, desperate patients are using Switzerland as a last resort for ending their misery.

In Switzerland a doctor can provide a patient who wants to die with lethal medication that the patient has to take by himself or herself.

Dr. Michael Irwin, a retired British doctor who paid to help a terminally ill patient commit suicide at a Swiss clinic, was the first person charged under new British guidelines for assisted dying. Dr. Irwin, who admitted he accompanied two other previous strangers to the Dignitas clinic to help them take their own lives, wants to make a test case out of his helping Raymond Cutkelvin to commit suicide. Cutkelvin, fifty-eight, a post office clerk from north London who was suffering from advanced pancreatic cancer, chose to die in the suicide clinic in February 2007.

Since then more Brits have been suspected of assisting in the suicides of loved ones. None has been prosecuted even though, technically, assisting a suicide is illegal for British citizens. If convicted of the crime, a person could face up to fourteen years in prison. The absence of prosecution stems from a 2009 House of Lords decision in favor of Debbie Purdy, who suffered from multiple sclerosis. She asked the court to clarify whether or not her husband would be prosecuted for helping her travel to Dignitas for an assisted suicide; it ruled that not knowing whether he would face charges is a violation of her human rights.

In late February 2010, British Director of Public Prosecutions Keir Starmer issued a list of conditions under which someone aiding a suicide might not be prosecuted. They include:

The victim had reached a voluntary, clear, settled, and informed decision to commit suicide.

The suspect was wholly motivated by compassion.

The actions of the suspect, although sufficient to come within the definition of the crime, were of only minor encouragement or assistance.

The suspect had sought to dissuade the victim from taking the course of action that resulted in his or her suicide.

The actions of the suspect may be characterised as reluctant encouragement or assistance in the face of a determined wish on the part of the victim to commit suicide.

The suspect reported the victim's suicide to the police and fully assisted them in their inquiries into the circumstances.

The above regulations might look a bit ridiculous, but they point to Britain's subtly making assisted suicide somehow legal without offending the religious industry.

Finally, it is my intention, if I become gravely ill, to choose either Dignitas or Exit International for assistance to say my final goodbye. Hopefully, by then, Australia will be mature enough and more secular, with the capability to rid itself of the vocal Christian lobby groups and the religious-right ide-ologies that are currently dominating its political and social scene. Hopefully, assisted suicide will be legalized, or at least the prohibition of the import of Nembutal will be lifted. (For more on Nembutal and other euthanasia drugs, see below.)

Exit International

PO Box 37781
Darwin NT 0821
Australia
Phone (Australian Reception): 1300 10 3948 (EXIT)
Phone (Outside Australia): +612-8005-1197
E-mail: contact@exitinternational.net
Website: www.exitinternational.net

Exit International USA

PO Box 4250
Bellingham WA 98227
USA
Phone: 1-248-809-4435

Exit International Europe

PO Box 82
Arklow
Republic of Ireland
Phone: (+44) 02071-931-557

Exit International is a leading **end-of-life choices,** information, advocacy, and law reform organization cofounded by Dr. **Philip Nitschke,** PhD, MD. Exit International US is the publisher of a do-it-yourself methods guidebook called *The Peaceful Pill Handbook.* This book was developed for the elderly and those who are seriously ill and their families.

Dr. Nitschke became the first physician in the world to administer a legal, lethal voluntary injection under the short-lived Rights of the Terminally Ill Act of the Australian Northern Territory in 1996. He was born in 1947 in rural South Australia. He studied physics at the University of Adelaide and completed a PhD in laser physics at Flinders University in 1972. He founded Exit in 1997 after the Australian government overturned the Northern Territory's voluntary euthanasia law. Exit is registered as a nonprofit organization and operates with the help of an army of volunteers worldwide. It is considered one of the leading sources of information, activism, and political advocacy for voluntary euthanasia and assisted suicide. It runs free educational public meetings and safe exit seminars for people aged fifty and over and others who are seriously ill.

The most effective method for ending life recommended by Dr. Nitschke is the drug Nembutal (a brand name of the drug pentobarbital). Versions of Nembutal are legally available to veterinarians for euthanizing animals. In many countries it is illegal to import and use on humans for assisting suicide. Dr. Nitschke has been helping people obtain Nembutal from Mexico and other overseas sources since the late 1990s.

People have been able to pay Exit International for guidelines on how to obtain Nembutal since 2000. They can also download Exit's instructions from *The Peaceful Pill*

Handbook, which has been published online in the US since the drug was banned in some countries like Australia and New Zealand.

Unfortunately, to flout oppressive laws, many elderly people who are tired of life are forced to become drug runners to obtain Nembutal. Mexican regulations controlling the sale of Nembutal are lax. People are now aware that if they leave it until too late, their health won't allow them to make the trip. When it is too late, they turn to organizations like Exit International for help. Many people, however, are illegally buying the lethal drug of choice on the Internet from Mexico and receiving it by post without being detected by customs authorities. The buyers learned about this service from Dr. Nitschke's latest version of his banned *The Peaceful Pill Handbook*. Two bottles of the drug are most likely needed for a serene death, both costing approximately US$500. Each bottle of 100 milliliters contains six grams of Nembutal. When purchasing the drug on the black market, however, the cost is much more. Only the wealthy can afford it.

Ordering Nembutal online is the latest example of the risks some people are prepared to take to get the drug regarded by euthanasia proponents as the Holy Grail for those bent on suicide. Known as the *green dream*, Nembutal was once prescribed (in lower doses) as a sleeping aid. It is used for legal euthanasia in Europe and assisted suicide in the US and was the drug Dr. Nitschke used to help four people die in the Australian Northern Territory under the (now overturned) world's first euthanasia laws.

Besides Tijuana and other Mexican cities, Nembutal can be bought from locations such as Peru, Bolivia, Bangkok, and Beijing. People can take a cruise from San Diego, California, and stop off at a Mexican port to do their shopping for the drug, or they can go on an organized shopping trip. If possible find a taxi driver or street hawker who can speak some English.

Warning: Purchasing Nembutal on the Internet or on the black market is fraught with danger.

> First, it could be unreliable.
> Second, it is very costly.
> Third, it could be confiscated by customs.

People returning to their countries with the drug are keen to have their Nembutal tested to check its efficacy—something Exit International is starting to do. The safest way to do this is to deal with any not-for-profit pro-euthanasia organizations, some of which are discussed here. Their addresses and phone numbers are as shown.

As was reported on September 26, 2011 by *Adelaide News*, Dr. Philip Nitschke has gained permission to import Nembutal to provide it to two women who are category-A patients, or people who are expected to die within a few months.

The drug is provided to patients with clear instructions: it is to help them sleep. If they breach those instructions, they are made aware, there are significant dangers. Patients also have to sign statutory notifications that they are aware of the risks associated with taking more than one tablet a night to help them sleep. It should be noted that one of the women who was suffering from motor-neurone disease was treated by another doctor.

Dr. Nitschke has said there is not much doubt Nembutal is the best end-of-life drug. It is similar to what Judy Garland and Marilyn Monroe used when they committed suicide.

Pentobarbital, a short-acting barbiturate, was first synthesized in 1928. It is used in the US state of Oregon for physician-assisted suicide and is by the Swiss euthanasia group Dignitas. In the Netherlands a pentobarbital elixir is used for physician-assisted suicide. The drug is also approved for use in executions in the US states of Oklahoma, Arizona, and Texas.

Hopefully soon, patients throughout the other so-called democratic, conservative, semi-secular Western countries will be provided with the drug. In the meantime the least these conservative countries must do is to make information about ending one's life publicly available. People must have the right of choice. They don't want to be deprived of information on how to take barbiturates. They don't want to go through all the trouble of travelling to other countries to obtain the drug where it is sold legally or on the black market. Countries banning a publication such as *The Peaceful Pill Handbook*, which is available through Exit, are acting against their citizens' democratic rights. It is the right of every individual to decide if he or she wants to take his or her own life.

Desperate patients would not resort to the help of pro-euthanasia organizations, such as Dignitas and Exit International, if it weren't for the gutless politicians who shirk their responsibility to make uniform laws with strict safeguards that allow euthanasia and assisted suicide.

Final Exit Network

PO Box 665
Pennington, NJ 08534
USA

Phone: (886) 654-9156
E-mail: info@finalexitnetwork.org

ERGO

24829 Norris Lane
Junction City, OR
USA
Phone: 97448-9559
E-mail: ergo@efn.org

One of the founding members and the current chairman of the Final Exit Network is Derek Humphry. He's been
involved for over thirty years in the fight for the cause, and
his published books on the subject have become synony-
mous with the fight for the legalization of euthanasia and assisted suicide as human rights and freedom of choice issues.
Humphry is also the founder of the Euthanasia Research and
Guidance Organization (ERGO).

Mentally competent adults have a basic human right
to end their lives when they suffer from fatal or irreversible illnesses or intractable pain, when their quality
of life is personally unacceptable, and when the future
holds only hopelessness and misery. Such a right should
be an individual choice, including the timing and place,
free of any restrictions by the law, clergy, medical professionals, even friends and relatives, no matter how
well-intentioned.

The Final Exit Network does not encourage anyone to
end his or her life, does not provide the means to do so, and
does not actively assist in a person's death. It does, however, support any member who requests it when medical

circumstances warrant the decision. Individual needs and timetables are evaluated and coordinated with the assigned Exit guide, who will provide the information on all alternatives for care at the end of life, including all legal methods of self-deliverance that will produce a peaceful, quick, certain, and painless death.

Although it is not mandatory, the patient is encouraged to use hospice care and to seek consultation with a psychiatrist, an oncologist, and/or other medical specialists.

Only members are accepted into the Exit guide program, which does the following:

> It offers free service to all who apply, provides relevant information, does home visits if possible, and offers compassionate counseling for individuals and families.
>
> It raises awareness among all Americans concerning this basic human right.
>
> It promotes the use of advance directives and other related legal instruments to document the intentions of any individual.
>
> It sponsors research into new peaceful and reliable methods to end life.
>
> It vigorously defends its guiding principle in a court of law when necessary.

The Final Exit Network is a tax-exempt, non-profit 501(c)(3) educational and research organization. As a non-profit organization, it depends on fully tax-deductible donations, memberships, and bequests to fund its many costly activities. There is no fee for its services.

Compassion & Choices

PO Box 101810
Denver, CO 80250
USA
Phone: 800-247-7421

Compassion & Choices offers end-of-life consultations for American citizens and provides information and support, but does not provide nor administer the means to aid dying.

Their counselors are passionate about understanding each individual situation. If appropriate they refer individuals to another organization that would best meet their needs. For those who meet their guidelines, they initiate more in-depth interviews to assess their needs, explain the process, and explore the options for dignified and peaceful death.

In addition to the above services, the end-of-life consultation team offers supportive counseling to individuals and their families and attempts to match them with volunteers and advocates for effective pain management. They assist with referrals to hospices and with planning for important health care decisions, such as advance directives, living wills, and the appointment of health care agents. They serve as a clearinghouse for information on grief, funerals, organ donation, support groups, and so on.

Dignity in Dying

181 Oxford Street
London, W1D 2JT
UK
Phone: 020 7479 7730
E-mail: info@dignityindying.org.uk

Dignity in Dying is a non-profit United Kingdom campaigning organization for individuals' freedom of choice and control over end-of-life decisions and the alleviation of pain and suffering. It campaigns on many medical and palliative services at the end of life, including providing terminally ill adults with the option of a painless, assisted death within strict legal safeguards. It is funded by voluntary contributions from members of the public. The organization declares it is independent of any political, religious, or other affiliations. It declares its campaign looks to bring about a more compassionate approach to the end of life.

It points out that in the 2010 British Social Attitudes survey, eighty-two percent of the general public believed a doctor should probably or definitely be allowed to end the lives of patients who are inflicted with painful, incurable diseases at their request. This was further analyzed to show seventy-one percent of religious people and ninety-two percent of nonreligious people supported this statement.

Alongside its campaigning work, Dignity in Dying, through its partner charity Compassion in Dying, is also an information source on end-of-life issues and a provider of advance directives. The group has repeatedly published opinion polls showing considerable public support for a change to the law on assisted dying and showing support from doctors and disabled people.

The group's interpretation of a dignified death is:

> Everybody should be able to choose where they die, who else would be present at that time, and the treatment options they would welcome or not. A person should have access to information on their end-of-life options from qualified experts, and their

caregivers, family, and friends should also be able to access high quality care and support. Individuals should have the right to plan for and then take personal control over their own death, including the medication and pain relief they wish to receive or not.

They encourage their supporters to campaign for a change to the current laws so terminally ill, mentally competent adults who feel their suffering has become unbearable can opt for assisted death, subject to strict rules and safeguards.

One of the group's main arguments is that their proposals for a comprehensive strategy around the issue of assisted dying would provide safeguards and protection for an individual from, for example, the coercive pressures to die that some people believe can be exerted by families of the frail or relatively disadvantaged. Dignity in Dying argues that at the moment not only can unscrupulous people do this in a relatively unchecked way, but the legal authorities can generally carry out investigations only after a person's death. Under the organization's plans, there would be safeguards and checks upfront to ensure a person is fully informed and counseled as to his or her rights and options and protected from possible malignant influences.

They argue that their proposals would alleviate a great deal of the stress and worry that approaching death can bring to a person, particularly one suffering significant pain from a terminal illness. The use of advance directives can help significantly, but they also believe that if a right to an assisted suicide is available, the very knowledge of this fact can alleviate many of the worries an individual might have.

The Dignity in Dying group is often opposed by religious believers and groups such as Care Not Killing. Many people of a religious persuasion take the views that all life is sacred and that only natural processes (and God) should determine a person's death. Dignity in Dying simply argues that if a person does not wish to take advantage of a change in the law that would allow for an assisted death, then that is down to personal choice. However, it strongly opposes those who would try to deny an individual the right to a personal choice in the matter by blocking enabling legislation. Meanwhile, opponents argue that the introduction of the sort of legislation supported by Dignity in Dying can be a slippery slope toward more draconian measures. Dignity in Dying refutes this by pointing out that the will of the government would be paramount, and any change in the law would be subject to ongoing review once established.

World Federation of Right to Die Societies
www.worldrtd.net
Libby Drake, WF Board Secretary
E-mail: wfsecretary@gmail.com

The federation was founded in 1980 and consists of forty-five right-to-die organizations from twenty-six countries. The federation believes individuals should have the right to make their own choices as to the manner and timing of their own deaths. Each of its member societies is working in its own way to secure this right. The federation provides an international link for organizations working to secure or protect the rights of individuals to self-determination at the ends of their lives.

It disseminates current information and educational materials about voluntary euthanasia, physician-assisted dying, other right-to-die issues, and related matters of interest. It promotes cooperation and liaising among its member societies and facilitates international conferences on dying and death. It provides assistance, where requested, to groups and individuals interested in establishing similar societies in countries where they do not currently exist, and responds to requests by interested groups, scholars, and individuals for information about right-to-die issues.

Its charter includes the independent choice of its member societies and the support of the member organizations in their work to achieve their own objectives. It does not require the member societies to adhere to a specific belief or goal other than supporting a person's right to a dignified death. The objectives and work of the member societies depends on existing laws within their countries and how they define the needs of individuals. Some of them work to promote laws for living wills or other advance medical directives while other societies focus on obtaining the legal right to physician aid in dying through either physician-assisted suicide or voluntary euthanasia.

Euthanasia Drugs

Warnings: First, the following information on drugs used in euthanasia and assisted suicide are dose-dependent and must only be prescribed or administered by qualified personnel. The doses are highly variable and dependent on the individual's physical characteristics.

Second, the information below was obtained from various sources, and its accuracy cannot be guaranteed. Readers should seek the opinion of a qualified person before embarking on any course of action.

Third, it is highly recommended, as a first port of call, patients embarking on euthanasia or assisted suicide should contact any convenient pro-euthanasia organizations in their country.

Pentobarbital: This is a short-acting barbiturate commonly sold under several names including Nembutal and Sedalphorte. It has been used in both animals and humans as a sedative, a hypnotic, an anticonvulsant, and an anesthetic. These drugs are available in both liquid and tablet forms and can be taken orally or intravenously depending on the dosage or formulation. The liquid form administered intravenously induces death faster than the tablet form taken orally.

Barbiturates are any group of drugs that depress brain functions. They act by depressing the central nervous system starting with the cerebral cortex, which causes rapid loss of consciousness progressing to anesthesia that induces respiratory and cardiac arrest. They are very effective anesthetic agents, free from distressing side effects, the application of which is considered the best practice for their rapid action, rapid loss of consciousness, and fast cardiac arrest. Above all they are relatively cheap.

Barbiturates are derived from barbituric acid ($C_4H_4N_2O_3$), a combination of urea and malonic acid. They have a sedative (tranquilizing), hypnotic (sleep-inducing), anticonvulsant, or anesthetic effect. In medical practice short-acting barbiturates are injected intravenously to induce rapid anesthesia before surgery.

Phenobarbitone, a long-acting barbiturate, is prescribed with other medicines to prevent epileptic seizures. Other barbituric-acid derivatives were used as anti-anxiety medications until the development of the tranquilizer. Euthanasia products are generally formulated to use barbiturates combined with an anesthetic agent. The best method of their application is intravenously. The oral applications in tablet or liquid forms have slower action and are best used for sedation before the intravenous injection.

Secobarbital Use in Oregon: Currently in Oregon secobarbital and Nembutal are the medications most commonly prescribed for physician-assisted suicide. They are proven to be the most effective and reliable medications. The lethal dose prescribed is typically nine grams of secobarbital in capsules or ten grams of pentobarbital liquid to be consumed at one time. The contents of the secobarbital capsules or the pentobarbital liquid should be mixed with a sweet substance such as juice to mask the bitter taste. Until the time of use, the medication must be stored out of reach of children and kept away from others to prevent unintentional overdose or abuse.

Patients are usually advised to take the lethal dose on an empty stomach to increase the rate of absorption. The typical dose of pentobarbital as an oral hypnotic for adults is 100 to 200 milligrams at bedtime; the dose of secobarbital is 100 milligrams orally at bedtime. Patients receiving the lethal dose of secobarbital or pentobarbital should take an antiemetic (e.g. metoclopramide) about one hour before ingesting the barbiturate to prevent nausea and vomiting. Cases of vomiting after taking an antiemetic have been reported; in the event of vomiting after medication ingestion, patients are instructed to have a family member contact the attending physician to determine the course of action. Also patients are instructed that if they decide not to end their life after ingesting the medication, they must contact emergency medical services to begin lifesaving measures.

Patients are informed of appropriate disposal methods in case the medication is not taken; the Food and Drug Administration provides guidance on that issue. Secobarbital and pentobarbital are not among the medications recommended for disposal by flushing. They should be placed in the household trash after mixing with an unpalatable substance such as coffee grounds. Unused medications also can be brought to a drug "take back" program run by law enforcement personnel. Patients are not permitted to return controlled-substance medications to a pharmacy.

KCl Poison Drug: The chemical compound potassium chloride (KCl) is a metal halide salt composed of potassium and chlorine. In its pure state, it is odorless and has a white or colorless vitreous crystal appearance. KCl is used in medicine, scientific applications, and food processing. Its formulation is intended to provide an extended release of potassium from the matrix to minimize the likelihood of producing high, localized concentrations of potassium within the gastrointestinal tract. It is odorless and has a saline taste. It is freely soluble in water and insoluble in alcohol.

KCl is methamphetamine, a powerful central nervous system stimulant. The drug works directly on the brain and spinal cord by interfering with normal neurotransmission. Neurotransmitters are chemical substances naturally produced within nerve cells that they use to communicate with each other and send messages to influence and regulate thinking and all other systems throughout the body. The main neurotransmitter affected by methamphetamine is dopamine, which is involved with the body's natural reward system.

A synthetic drug, methamphetamine has a high potential for abuse and dependence. It is illegally produced and sold in pill form, capsules, powder, and chunks. However, it is legally and commonly used by intravenous injection to euthanize animals after the application of general anesthetic. The drug is good for its rapid action by causing death by cardiac arrest. However, methamphetamine causes cardiac arrest without rendering the patient unconscious and can produce severe cardiac pain as a result. Sedation provides an insufficient analgesia to block painful side effects of the euthanasia agent and is considered unacceptable when used alone for euthanasia.

Methamphetamine short circuits a person's survival system by artificially stimulating the reward center or pleasure areas in the brain. This leads to increased confidence in meth and less confidence in the normal rewards of life. This happens on a physical level at first and then it affects the user psychologically. The result is decreased interest in other aspects of life while reliance and interest in meth increases. In one study laboratory animals pressed levers to release methamphetamine into their blood stream rather than eat, mate, or satisfy other natural drives. The animals died of starvation while giving themselves methamphetamine even though food was available.

Methamphetamine was developed in the last century from its parent drug amphetamine and was originally used in nasal decongestants and bronchial inhalers, and for the treatment of narcolepsy and obesity. In the 1970s methamphetamine became a drug with little medical use and a high potential for abuse. The drug is referred to by many names including, meth, speed, go-fast, zip, and cristy. Pure methamphetamine hydrochloride, the smokable form of the drug, is called LA or ice. Since the 1980s ice has been smuggled from Taiwan and South Korea into Hawaii, where its use became widespread by 1988.

Asphyxiation

The most popular gases used for asphyxiation are carbon monoxide, nitrogen, helium, and argon. The principle behind the effectiveness of any device used is oxygen deprivation that leads to hypoxia (the starvation of body cells and tissues from oxygen), asphyxia (a lack of air/suffocation), and death within minutes. They are slower acting than the previous methods. However, in high concentrations they can be effective. To avoid distress the method is usually used after general anesthetic.

Carbon monoxide is often used by people committing suicide by diverting a car's exhaust system into a sealed car. It was also one of Dr. Jack Kevorkian's methods using a machine called a Mercitron ("mercy machine"). The device employed a face gas mask fed by a canister of carbon monoxide. A valve would be released to start the gas flowing. Depending on the person's disability, a makeshift handle could be attached to the valve to make it easier to turn. Or, with the valve in the open position, a clip or clothespin could be clamped on the tubing. Pulling it off would allow the gas to flow. According to Kevorkian, this method took ten minutes or longer. Sometimes he encouraged people to take sedatives or muscle relaxants to keep them calm as they breathed deeply.

Death by hypoxia is a slow process, with a time variable for losing consciousness, and it can cause distressing side effects. It requires a pure source of carbon monoxide as impurities in the gas can cause irritation, which makes it unacceptable for euthanasia.

Nitrogen is commonly used by Exit International for euthanasia. Dr. Philip Nitschke invented a delivery device in 2008 using an ordinary barbecue-gas bottle filled with nitrogen, a plastic suicide bag, and some plastic tubing with one end attached to the gas canister and the other fixed inside the bag by a tie held by adhesive tape. In December 2008 Nitschke released details of the euthanasia device to the media. The new device was a modification of the earlier exit bag plus helium method described in *The Peaceful Pill Handbook*. Instead of using a prepackaged, disposable cylinder of helium, he suggested filling purchased empty LPG cylinders (rated at 3300 kPa) with compressed nitrogen and then regulating them with a jet assembly to give a flow of around ten liters per minute into the standard plastic exit bag (*see below). This equipment has some small advantages over the helium method because larger amounts of nitrogen are available and flow rates last longer. Also the gas is more physiological; with no chance of adverse reaction (helium is reported to cause some twitching during death).

If there is any leakage of nitrogen from the cylinder in the period of storage, it can be topped up at any time to the recommended 400 pounds per square inch (2,800 kPa). The helium party-balloon cylinders cannot be refilled and, if they leak over time, must be discarded.

Nitschke called this process flawless and undetectable as it uses ordinary household products available from hardware stores. Inhaling the pure nitrogen, patients lose consciousness in approximately twelve seconds and die a few minutes later.

According to Nitschke nitrogen is extremely quick; no other drugs are needed; it is reliable, peaceful, and readily available; and it is undetectable. If helium is used new autopsy tests can detect it.

* An exit bag (or suicide bag) is a device consisting of a large plastic bag with a draw cord. It is usually used to commit suicide in conjunction with nitrogen. It makes the method of death difficult to trace if the bag and gas canister are removed before the death is reported. This is recommended by right-to-die groups and on the Internet as a certain, fast, and painless suicide method.

Other Methods

The Thanatron: Invented by Dr. Jack Kevorkian, the device involved an individual pushing a button that released drugs or chemicals that would end the person's life. Two deaths were assisted by this device, which had three canisters or bottles mounted on a metal frame about six inches (150 mm) wide by eighteen inches (460 mm) high. Each bottle had a syringe that connected to a single intravenous (IV) line in the person's arm. The first bottle contained ordinary saline or salt water. Another contained a sleep-inducing barbiturate called sodium thiopental, and the third held a lethal mixture of potassium chloride, which immediately stops the heart, and pancuronium bromide, a muscle relaxant to prevent spasms during the dying process.

> <u>First</u>, a doctor begins the saline solution flow.
> <u>Second</u>, the person who wants to die delivers the barbiturates by activating a switch (pushing a button or pulling a string).
> <u>Third</u>, either a timer goes off or a mechanical device is triggered by the person's falling arm as the drugs take effect, and that starts the lethal drug flowing.

The idea is for the deadly chemicals to enter the bloodstream only after the person is asleep. Death usually occurs within two minutes.

Unfortunately, Kevorkian brought harm to the euthanasia and assisted suicide causes with his challenges to the authorities and the medical profession instead of worrying about the patients. He used the deaths of his patients for publicity and in the process generated negative debate and provoked religious ethicists to highlight the danger of legalizing euthanasia and assisted suicide, especially because his method lacked the safeguards that could prevent possible abuse.

The Deliverance Machine: Invented by Dr. Philip Nitschke, this device consisted of a notebook computer and software called Deliverance, which asked the patient a series of questions and automatically administered a lethal injection of barbiturates if the correct answers were made. Even if it would have been legally possible for a doctor to administer a lethal injection, Dr. Nitschke preferred the patient initiated the process. The machine also allowed a doctor to leave the patient with members of the family when the button was pushed.

Terminally ill patients used it to end their lives with lethal doses of drugs after they answered "yes" to a series of questions on the laptop screen. This procedure was legal in Australia's Northern Territory between 1995 and 1997.

Lethal Injection and US Executions: As discussed earlier the practice of injecting a person with a fatal dose of drugs (typically a barbiturate, paralytic, and potassium solution) is for the express purpose of causing the immediate death of the subject. The main application for this procedure is capital punishment, but the term may also be applied in a broad sense to euthanasia and suicide. It kills the person first by putting him or her to sleep, then by stopping the breathing and heart (in that order).

The condemned person is strapped onto a carriage; two intravenous lines are inserted, one in each arm. Only one is necessary to carry out the execution—the other is a backup in the event the primary line fails. A line leading from the IV in an adjacent room is attached and secured to the prisoner's IV and secured so the line does not snap during the injections.

Following connection of the lines, saline drips are started in both arms. This too is standard medical procedure. It must be ascertained that the IV lines are easily seen and protected; ensuring the chemicals do not mix in the IV lines and occlude the needle, preventing the drugs from reaching the offender. A heart monitor is attached so prison officials can monitor when death has occurred.

The intravenous injection is usually a series of drugs given in a set sequence, designed first to induce unconsciousness followed by death through paralysis of respiratory muscles and/or by cardiac arrest through depolarization of cardiac muscle cells.

The execution of the condemned in most states involves three separate injections (in sequential order):

> First, sodium thiopental (better known as sodium pentothal) or pentobarbital is an ultra-short action barbiturate and an anesthetic agent capable of rendering the prisoner unconscious in a few seconds.
>
> Second, pancuronium bromide, a non-depolarizing muscle relaxant that causes complete, fast, and sustained paralysis of the skeletal striated muscles, including the diaphragm and the rest of the respiratory muscles. This would eventually cause death by asphyxiation.
>
> Third, potassium chloride stops the heart and thus causes death by cardiac arrest.

In Belgium and the Netherlands, pancuronium is recommended in the protocol for euthanasia. After administering sodium thiopental to induce coma, pancuronium is delivered in order to stop breathing.

The most common anesthetic for the loss of consciousness and to provide acceptable analgesia and muscle relaxation is Tietamine-Zolazepam, a drug combination for intravenous injection that is professionally administered. Other drugs used for acceptable results are Thiopentone and Propofol. Combinations of pre-euthanasia drugs, such as Ketamine and Butorphanol, are often chosen to render the body insensible to the pain that may result from some euthanasia methods. When using a combination of drugs, doctors usually ensure a sufficient dose of each drug is used and sufficient time is allowed for them to reach their maximum effect before euthanasia is undertaken. These drugs are sometimes used for painless euthanasia when expertly given intravenously as overdoses.

Starvation and dehydration: Starvation is a severe reduction in vitamin, nutrient, and energy intake. It is the most extreme form of malnutrition. In humans, prolonged starvation can cause permanent organ damage and eventual death. Dehydration is a gradual process. The body loses water through urination, perspiration, and breath. After several days, the volume of blood in the body begins to decline because of the lack of water and the concentrations of toxins and carbon dioxide in the blood increases. All of the body's systems gradually become weaker.

After about ten days, organ systems begin to fail. The kidneys and liver may stop filtering toxins from the blood. The muscles that drive breathing begin to fail. When the heart is deprived of oxygen, it stops beating.

There are conflicting opinions regarding the humaneness of this process. Some paint a picture of dehydration as a gentle process while others consider it as a cruel, inhumane, and even agonizing death.

Some physicians describe dehydration as follows:

- As dehydration begins, there is extreme thirst, dry mouth, and thick saliva. The patient becomes dizzy, faint, and unable to stand or sit and experiences severe cramping in the arms and legs due to the sodium and potassium concentrations in the body going up as fluids go down. In misery the patient tries to cry but there are no tears. The patient experiences severe abdominal cramps, nausea, and dry heaving as the stomach and intestines dry out.

- By now the skin and lips are cracking and the tongue is swollen. The nose may bleed as the mucous membranes dry out and break down. The skin loses elasticity, thins, and wrinkles. The hands and feet become cold as the remaining fluids in the circulatory system are shunted to the vital organs in an attempt to stay alive. The person stops urinating and has severe headaches as the brain shrinks from lack of fluids. The patient becomes anxious but then gets progressively more lethargic.
- Some patients have hallucinations and seizures as their body chemistry becomes even more imbalanced. This proceeds to coma before death occurs. The final event as the blood pressure becomes almost undetectable is a major heart arrhythmia that stops the heart from pumping.

Other physicians describe starvation and dehydration differently:

- The cessation of eating and drinking is the dominant way mammals die. It is a very gentle way that nature has provided for animals to leave this life. After twenty-four hours without any food, the body goes into a different mode and the person is not hungry anymore. Total starvation is not painful or uncomfortable at all. When humans were hunting rabbits millions of years ago, they had to have a backup mode because they didn't always get a rabbit and they can't go hunting if they are hungry. The basic cause of starvation is an imbalance between energy intake and energy expenditure. In other words the body expends more energy than it takes in as food. This imbalance can arise from one or more medical conditions and/or circumstantial situations.

- On March 21, 2005 *The New York Times* cited Dr. Sean Morrison, a professor of geriatrics and palliative care at Mount Sinai School of Medicine in New York, who insisted starvation victims "generally slip into a peaceful coma."

Psychiatrist Dr. Stanley A. Terman, in his book *The Best Way to Say Goodbye: A Legal Peaceful Choice at the End of Life*, describes one of the methods of ending life: the refusal of tube feeding. Refusing fluids and tube feeding is legal and was done by Ruth Bell Graham, the wife of preacher Billy Graham, before she died. Generally, in many Western countries, the refusal of fluids and tube feeding gives terminally ill patients the opportunity to change their minds if they decide not to end their lives.

Terman's book provides accurate information from legal, medical, psychological, and ethical perspectives. The book is supported by clinical and medical ethicist professor Dr. Ronald Miller and attorney and social worker Michael Evans. It deals with the process of dying but not death. It provides a description of a legal and peaceful method of dying for most of those who suffer from devastating terminal conditions such as permanent brain damage or incurable, progressive dementia.

Remember that in Terri Schiavo's case, the feeding tube was removed after she was in a coma for fifteen years and following a lengthy court battle. Terri's parents requested

Dr. Terman help them determine if Terri really wanted to continue tube feeding, and his declaration was included in the court case.

Final Word

Many sick people take their own lives when they are still relatively healthy because they fear their illnesses will make them incapable of doing it later. Denying people the right to die may cause them to commit suicide when they are still in reasonable health. Many terminally ill people are prepared to do anything to end their lives. Some of them die in terrible, violent ways or alone. It is a tragedy for them and their families, and it could be avoidable if politicians were free to produce laws without being hampered by undemocratic, vocal, ultraconservative theologians and the religious-right minority.

Some politicians in some of the so-called secular countries are not only influenced but also controlled by aggressive religious lobby groups. Despite the fact that surveys consistently show over seventy percent of believers and nonbelievers alike are in favor of legal, voluntary euthanasia and assisted suicide, gutless politicians, in fear of religious backlash, are reluctant to act. The majority is in favor of euthanasia and assisted suicide simply because everyone knows someone (a parent, grandparent, relative, or friend) who is terminally ill and near death and suffering unbearable pain. The only solution left for these helpless patients is to pass away peacefully and painlessly.

Legal **death by choice** is a personal right of everyone who desperately needs it, and it is the most important final right anyone may one day have to exercise. Gravely ill people have the right to decide what to do with their lives. The terminally ill and victims of severe accidents should never be under pressure to stay alive no matter what. Legally safeguarded euthanasia and assisted suicide are necessary as a counterbalance to ever more exotic techniques for prolonging life, which seem to have little regard for its quality. Some may argue it is immoral to take life; many others would argue it is immoral to extend it when it has lost its meaning and is no longer tolerable.

The religious industry has always, either subtly or overtly, acted as a stumbling block against freedom of choice and democratic rights and tended to force its dogmatic beliefs on everyone else. Religious-right groups achieve their objectives by pushing politicians to act as surrogates for the implementation of their social and political agendas. Furthermore, they attack the senses of average people with the emotion of hope and the fear of God by prompting the naïve to react as if they have moral obligations to follow their dogmas, which are based on speculations rather than facts.

In secular democracy religious beliefs are the privilege of the believer, provided they are not made an issue in the political domain. The entitlement to religious beliefs should never be extended into a legal demand imposed on everyone else. Imposing religious dogmas on others destroys the concept of secular democracy.

An extreme confusion and bad consequence of religious influence and apathetic public behavior is that end-of-life decisions are left up to medical staff and practitioners. Doctors are in the unenviable position of having to break existing inadequate laws for the sakes of suffering patients. This is most unfair to them, and it is unfair to the patients who are left lingering at death's door for lack of across-the-board response by politicians and medical associations. Medicine should never be influenced by religion or forced to be used as a primary objective to prolong life with an aggressive approach. Instead, the use of medicine should be guided by the concept of giving patients comfort and reducing their suffering.

In promoting falsehood and fear of the slippery slope and the imperfection of safeguards associated with euthanasia and assisted suicide, the religious industry is ignoring the fact that throughout human life nothing has been perfect. An example of that is having a heart attack or a stroke or just belonging to a religious sect that is at war with other sects. Maybe the biggest risk for some people is going to church and getting brainwashed. The case studies of voluntary euthanasia in the Netherlands and assisted suicide in Oregon come very near being perfect systems, and these should be copied throughout the civilized world.

A democratic **death by choice** in a secular society can only be achieved by ignoring the fear generated by ultraconservative theologians and by getting politicians to resist the blackmail of losing votes due to irrational religious hysteria. Civilized Western countries should embrace a combination of the three models of end-of-life care: the Oregon model for assisted suicide, the Netherlands model for euthanasia, and a new palliative care model that includes physician-assisted suicide.

Furthermore, civilized countries should provide doctors with specific training in all aspects of passive and active euthanasia and the protocols of their administration. The training must form part of their university studies and hospital residencies. It must be introduced as soon as possible, as the demand for the service will trump the religious resistance to it. The demand for the service is driving people to seek underground acquisition of lethal drugs and help from friendly doctors or mercy killings by partners or friends. This will sooner or later provoke further activism to force gutless politicians to act positively and produce laws that coincide with public sentiment. Furthermore, the spread of covert sales of euthanasia drugs, especially on the Internet with its associated problems, will have huge social and political consequences.

The people who are suffering or have suffered without the respite of a legally sanctioned **death by choice** hopefully in the near future can escape the mind-boggling effects of religious mumbo jumbo and reject all those acting as stumbling blocks to its introduction. The ultraconservative theologians, with their lack of compassion for humans in desperate circumstances and for people who do not have the power or means to end their misery, should be held in contempt. As should their self-righteous idea that saving the so-called immortal souls outweighs their rightful duty to others. We should also despise their undemocratic way of shifting the debate from power and influence to power and control and of forcing their oppressive ideologies on everyone.

The unfortunate outcome of tangling religion with politics is that, for legal and religious reasons, doctors abandon their patients at a crucial stage. It destroys the honesty and trust in medical treatment.

The religious industry believes God gave his people free will, yet they insist on forbidding people from using it. Ultraconservative religious fanatics must stop the fascism against terminally ill people who want to die with dignity. The terminally ill who are nearing death deserve to exercise their democratic, human rights and freedom of choice openly, not by underground methods.

Euthanasia and assisted suicide are not only about intolerance to pain or being a burden on loved ones or the fear of dying without dignity; they are also about the loss of autonomy, the loss of the ability to engage in activities that make life enjoyable, and the loss of control of bodily functions.

It should be easy to agree that everyone is entitled to die in the way that fits his or her beliefs.

Acknowledgments

Many prolific writers have dealt with the complex issues of euthanasia and assisted suicide. Here in my book I want to add to their voices, participate with their activism, and acknowledge their enormous contributions to the debate, which is currently being hijacked by the religious industry with slogans designed to swing public opinion against citizens' legitimate democratic and human rights. Hopefully, through the writing and campaigning of enlightened and prominent people, the wheel of reason will turn to rid the world of dogmas based on conjecture rather than a scientific foundation. Prominent writers and activists who directly or indirectly advocate the legalization of euthanasia and assisted suicide are in effect taking a stand against ultraconservative theologians who want to impose their ideologies on everyone else.

Derek Humphry, the author of *Final Exit*, is one of those writers and activists who don't hesitate to declare their antireligious stand to bring about change and to make end-of-life choices legal. Humphry has a history of more than thirty years and a long list of achievements as a fighter for the legalization of voluntary euthanasia and physician-assisted suicide for terminally ill people. He is dedicated to the cause of allowing peaceful ends for dying people.

My intention is to follow a similar path—to serve not only the cause of suffering people but my own cause if I become gravely ill or in a vegetative state. My goal is to add my voice to the voices of people I admire, especially the ones who never hesitate to confront the vocal religious-right minority that attempts to impose its views on the silent majority.

It is my intention to add my own modest contribution to the debate with this book's different perspective. The book is in opposition to ultraconservative theologians behind the fanatic pro-life and right-to-life movements whose aim is to deny the majority the legitimate right of choice and to trample democratic and human rights.

Writers, advocates, and activists, especially those who speak through direct observation or personal experience with losing patients or loved ones as a result of terminal illness, deserve our respect and admiration for their courage to tell the world about it. We should always be thankful for the work and activism of Derek Humphry, Robert Orfali, Timothy Quill, Philip Nitschke, Ian Dowbiggin, Stanley Terman, David Nicholls, Gerald Dworkin, and many others who have devoted their lives and energy to a good cause.

This book is dedicated to them and to the terminally ill people who are unnecessarily suffering and deserve humane and merciful endings of their lives.

Last but not least, I wish to extend my thanks to the **CreateSpace team** for their excellent editing, formatting, interior design, artwork, production, publication, and promotion of this book. Their diligence and professionalism are very much appreciated. It is always a delight to deal with so many nice and dedicated people. **Thank you all!**

Sources

Encyclopedia Britannica
Encyclopedia Microsoft Encarta
Encyclopedia of Drugs and Addictive Substances
Medical and Health Encyclopedia
Medline Plus-Medical Encyclopedia
MedicineNet.com
Wikipedia
The Bible
Derek Humphry, *Final Exit: The Practicalities of Self-Deliverance and Assisted Suicide for the Dying*, 3rd Edition; New York: Dell Publishing; November 26, 2002
Derek Humphry, *Liberty and Death: A Manifesto Concerning an Individual's Right to Choose to Die*, March 23, 2009
Hani Montan, *Thorny Opinion*; Charleston, SC: BookSurge; 2008
Hani Montan, *Israel vs. America vs. the World*; Charleston, SC: CreateSpace; 2011

Stephen Hawking and Leonard Mlodinow, *The Grand Design*; New York: Bantam Books; 2010

Stephen Hawking, *A Brief History of Time*; New York: Bantam Books; 1988

David Filkin, *Stephen Hawking's Universe*; London: BBC Worldwide Publishing; 1997

Sarah Graham, Anne Hampshire, Elizabeth Hindmarsh, Barbara Squires and Sharon Wall, *My Health, My Future, My Choice*: 3rd edition; Advance Care Directive Association Inc.; 2010

Adelaidenews.com.au, September 26, 2011; "Dr. Philip Nitschke wins right to use euthanasia drug"

Rev. Dr. Andrew Dutney, *Monash Bioethics Review*, Vol. 16 No. 2, dated April 1997

Dr. Stanley A. Terman, *The Best Way to Say Goodbye: A Legal Peaceful Choice at the End of Life*; California: Life Transitions Publications; November 28, 2007

Dr. Philip Nitschke and Fiona Stewart, *The Peaceful Pill Handbook*; Exit International U.S. Ltd.; December 1, 2010

Dr. Ranjana Srivastava, *Tell Me the Truth: Conversation with My Patients about Life and Death*; Australia: Penguin Group; 2010

Robert Orfali, *Death with Dignity: The Case for Legalizing Physician-Assisted Dying and Euthanasia*; Mill City Press, Inc.; April 15, 2011

Timothy E. Quill, *Death and Dignity: Making Choices and Taking Charge*; W.W. Norton & Company; May 17, 1994

Ian Dowbiggin, *A Merciful End: The Euthanasia Movement in Modern America* (1st edition); US: Oxford University Press; January 9, 2003

Louisa Tasker, *Methods for the Euthanasia of Dogs and Cats: Comparison and Recommendations*; London: World Society for the Protection of Animals

Dworkin, R.G. Frey and Sissela Bok, *Euthanasia and Physician-Assisted Suicide (For and Against)*; UK: Cambridge University Press; August 28, 1998

Serita Stevens and Anne Bannon, *HowDunit—The Book of Poisons*; Ohio: Writers Digest Books; January 9, 2007

Dr. Geo Stone, *Suicide and Attempted Suicide*; New York: Carroll & Graf Pub; 2001.

www.ingramcontent.com/pod-product-compliance
Lightning Source LLC
Chambersburg PA
CBHW061345280526
45784CB00001B/144